South African Passage

"Life is its own journey,
presupposes its own change and movement,
and one tries to arrest them at one's eternal peril."

Sir Laurens van der Post

South African Passage

Diaries of the Wilderness Leadership School

Preface by Laurens van der Post
Introduction by Ian Player

Edited by Elizabeth Darby Junkin

FULCRUM, INC.
GOLDEN, COLORADO
1987

Wildlife Illustrations by
Nola Steele

Cover and Book Design
by Chris Bierwirth

Library of Congress Cataloging-in-Publication Data

South African Passage
1. Wildlife refuges — South Africa — Miscellanea.
2. Wilderness areas — South Africa — Miscellanea.
3. Outdoor life — South Africa — Miscellanea.
4. Wilderness Leadership School (South Africa)
I. Player, Ian
II. Wilderness Leadership School (South Africa)
QH77.S62S69 1987   508.68   86-25752
ISBN 1-55591-009-2

Printed in the United States of America

CONTENTS

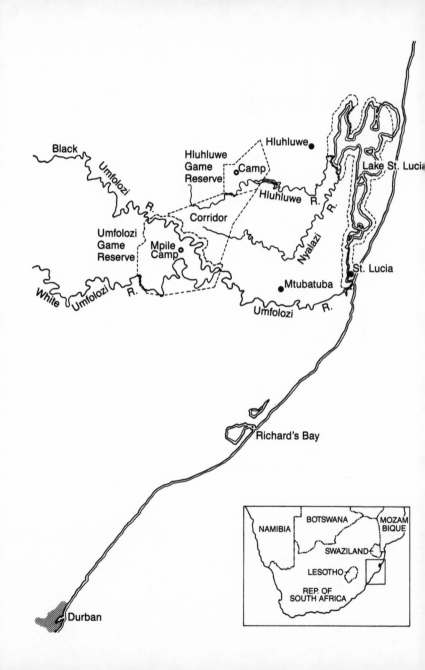

Preface

"Life is its own journey, presupposes its own change and movement, and one tries to arrest them at one's eternal peril . . ."
Venture to the Interior

I wrote those thoughts 35 years ago, when embarking upon a journey of my own into the great, primeval wilderness of Africa. It was long before I had ever presupposed the existence of a Wilderness Leadership School, or the vision of an Ian Player in guiding young people into the wilderness. Yet today I find that the idea fits anew a time, place and circumstance, and bespeaks a spirit of discovery and wilderness which is of critical importance if mankind is ever to find itself. For we are each still on that journey to find the wilderness within ourselves, and when we journey into the wilderness, we are able to touch the balance of that natural person which we know lives within us.

Those of us who have spent time in wilderness are aware of the fact that there is something more to wilderness than we ourselves can express. This is rooted perhaps in the effect that wilderness has on human beings who have become estranged from nature, who live in industrialised environments and are estranged in a sense from their natural selves. Wilderness has a profound impact on them, as well as on those of us more familiar with it.

I can perhaps illustrate this best by the example of three boys of different families and different nationalities, whose parents regarded them as "problem sons." All three boys had very privileged backgrounds, but somehow they couldn't come to terms with their own environments and with their own futures. Their parents came to me and asked what they could do to help their sons, because schools, doctors and educationalists did not seem to help. And I found a strange aboriginal voice in me saying, "Send them to the wilderness." I persuaded their parents to send them out to Zululand, where they went on a wilderness trail with Ian Player. Nothing was said to them about themselves. All they had was the mirror which nature presented to them, and through this experience, which had a profound psychological impact on them, they found something of themselves, something to do with their natural selves and the wilderness within. They returned to Europe and to their schools and universities, and today all three are creative citizens distinguishing themselves in the world.

How is it that the individual finds a sense of himself, a sense of home, in the wilderness? Why is it we have lost our sense of belonging in this other, rational world of ours? It seems as if we need to be conscious of the relationship between that within us that gives us our values, and that which makes us instinctively turn to and serve wilderness. To our development as individuals and as a human race this relationship is as crucial as it is mysterious. Yet somehow we have lost this sense of wonder, this feeling of belonging in this world of ours. The study of European history, the civilisation from which most of our values derive, indicates that gradually there has arisen a great cataclysmic divide within human nature. As we have become rational we have lost touch with our primitive nature, and as a result have lost touch with the sense of being known and of belonging. This divide has meant a loss of meaning in our hearts and minds. This is where we stand today. This is what wilderness is all about — a crisis of meaning in the modern world.

I believe that there is a fundamental and interdependent relationship — the greater the divide, the greater the loss of meaning, and the loss of a sense of direction in life. And this great divide is what has arisen between the rational, consciously oriented in us and that which is symbolised by the wilderness within us. Surely this quality of spirit tries to communicate to us day and night, through all that is instinctive and natural within us, offering a message of identity and meaning. Somehow those who have experienced being exposed to wilderness, who have taken people into the wild areas and lived with them there, have witnessed a change within them. Somehow they emerge from the wilderness transformed as if they were coming from a highly sacred atmosphere.

Wilderness is an instrument for enabling us to recover our

lost capacity for religious experience. The religious area is far more than just the Church. If you look at the history of Europe since Christ, you will see that the Church has tended to be caught up, as it is today, in the social problems of its time, and to be less than the religion it serves. The churches and the great cathedrals are really, in the time scale of human history, just tents on the journey somewhere else.

What wilderness does is present us with a blueprint, as it were, of what creation was about in the beginning, when all the plants and trees and animals were magnetic, fresh from the hands of whatever created them. This blueprint is still there, and those of us who see it find an incredible nostalgia rising in us, an impulse to return and discover it again. It is as if we are obeying that one great voice which resounds and resounds through the *Upanishads* of India: "O man, remember."

Through wilderness we remember and are brought home again. I believe this is what Ian Player does each time he introduces a young person to the wilderness and thus to himself. And I believe we, too, can take hope from this journey.

Sir Laurens van der Post
1987

Introduction
Wilderness: Trail to the Future

South Africa is part of the continent of Africa.

It is difficult, even for an American, to understand the vastness of Africa until he realizes that the United States will fit into Africa twice, with room to spare. It is a continent that has excited the interest of the developed world, from the time of the Greeks and the Romans. It was a Roman who said *Ex Africa semper alquid novi*: Out of Africa always something new.

The thoughts of the young people expressed in this book are examples of the response wild Africa evokes in the human soul. They are an expression of the transformation that takes place in the wilderness. Many people who come to discover Africa discover more about themselves because Africa in a way mirrors part of the human psyche.

It was true with David Livingstone, the great explorer, who travelled from Kuruman in the Cape Province of South Africa to the thunderous falls he named after Queen Victoria, then to the great lakes of Central Africa. Winston Churchill as a young man fought with the British Army in the Sudan, explored part of the country of Uganda and was a war correspondent in the Anglo-Boer War of 1899-1902. He expresses his feelings about Africa in many of his writings, and particularly recalls riding with the British troops on the highveld of South Africa and sleeping out at night under that brilliant southern sky. It was to remain for him a special memory all his life.

President Theodore Roosevelt tramped and hunted in Africa, and recorded his impressions in his book *African Game Trails*. In the Introduction the reader sees in an instant what a dramatic impact Africa made upon this man who did so much for the cause of conservation in America. He begins with a quote from Shakespeare, "I speak of Africa and golden joys," and he describes the country with, ". . . lakes like seas . . . mighty rivers rushing out of the heart of the continent through the sadness of endless marches; forests of gorgeous beauty, where death broods in dark and silent depths. . . . These things can be told. But there are no words that can tell the hidden spirit of the wilderness, that can reveal its mystery, its melancholy, and its charm." Again one hears the resonance of Africa within the psyche.

Carl Gustav Jung, the Swiss psychoanalyst who explored the soul of modern man, also travelled to Africa, where he discovered hidden depths within himself that had important bearing on his life's work as a psychiatrist and philosopher. While travelling on a train he awoke at dawn, which is symbolic in itself, and looked out of the window to see a black man, standing motionless, leaning on a long spear. Jung said he had the feeling that he had already experienced this moment and had always known this world which was separated from him only by distance in time. "It was as if I were this moment returning to the land of my youth, and as if I knew that dark-skinned man had been waiting for me for 5,000 years." He goes on to say, "I could not guess what string within myself was plucked at the sight of the solitary dark hunter. I only know that his world had been mine for countless millennia."

Africa was not left alone to go its own slow rhythmic way. The dark side of European man saw the continent as a place to be ravished, its gold, diamonds, timber and other precious natural resources there for the pickings. It was colonised, sometimes in the most ruthless fashion. France, Germany, Belgium, Holland, Portugal, Britain, Italy, they all carved up the continent, drawing lines on maps and ignoring tribal boundaries. America was guilty too of this domination of a continent, because she encouraged and accepted slavery. But in the last 40 years Africa has been decolonised, sometimes leaving in its wake misery, hunger and mayhem, and a refusal of some former colonial powers to take responsibility for what they created and the anticipations they aroused.

The Republic of South Africa consists of the land from the Limpopo River to the Cape of Good Hope. It is unique in that it has the largest white population on the African continent: some 5 million whites in a land of 30 million blacks, 3 million coloureds (people of mixed blood), 1 million Asians and a small number of Chinese. It is a country of great complexity that never fails to perplex the serious visitor. The whites are divided into 60 percent Afrikaans-speaking people descended from the Dutch who first colonised the Cape of Good Hope, and 40 percent English-speaking people who

are, in the main, descendents of British settlers of the 1820s
and 1840s and 1950s. However, amongst the English-speaking group are Italians, Portuguese, French, Germans and Scan-
dinavians. There is a big divergence in attitudes between the
Afrikaans and the English-speaking groups. The Afrikaners
have been in government for the past 38 years, bitterly
opposed by the majority of English-speakers. The bitterness
dates back to the Anglo-Boer War when the Afrikaners
were badly treated by the British government of the day.
The black people are composed of many different nations and
tribes, the Zulu nation being the biggest with 6 million people and a leader, in Chief Buthelezi, who is recognized inter-
nationally as one of the great statesmen in Africa. Following
the Zulus are 5 million Xhosas people, who in turn are followed by numerically smaller Sotho and Tswana people.
Two former British colonies, Lesotho and Swaziland, are
independent but completely surrounded by the Republic of
South Africa.

South Africa is both a First World and a Third World
country. Its mining industry is one of the most advanced in
the world. It has a network of paved roads unequalled in Africa and in many other countries too. It has the largest gold
fields in the world and is the biggest supplier of platinum
and chrome, minerals vital to the western world. It has vine-
yards and wineries as well as the biggest oil-from-coal
factories in the world. Alongside these developments, which
were made possible by the work of all the people of South

Africa, are poverty-stricken tribal areas and urban townships where life is a terrible and dangerous struggle.

South Africa is a troubled land but it has been so ever since the first settlers arrived in the Cape in 1652. Some of the worst wars the continent has experienced took place in South Africa, between black and black, white and black, and white and white. The earth of southern Africa has absorbed more than its share of human blood. It is a country struggling for identity, while at the same time each group within the country wants its own identity too. The western world has focussed on South Africa with increasing intensity in recent years. This focus is a combination of the aftermath of colonisation and the guilt it arouses, as well as a genuine concern with the insensitivity of the South African government over many issues. But what government is ever sensitive? There are, however, more South Africans than outsiders who are deeply concerned, as they should be because they live here.

The truth is that South Africa needs the world and resents being the pariah when there are other countries that equally, if not more so, deserve the pariahdom. The world needs South Africa not only for its gold, diamonds, platinum and chrome but also because it is a microcosm of our world. Deep in their hearts most people know that if South Africa cannot sort out its problems, neither will the world be able to do so. There are many evil people in South Africa who would not hesitate to see it become a second Lebanon if they thought they could rule over the rubble, but I believe there are more good than evil people, and the good ones are striving to keep the country on an even keel and provide a better future for all its inhabitants. For my own part, I think that the ecological problems of soil erosion and overpopulation and the rapidly diminishing wild lands are far more serious in the long term than the political situation, although I know the two are linked.

I am a South African born and bred. My great-grandfather on the paternal side came to Natal in 1850 from Gloucestershire in England. He married my great-grandmother, who was an Afrikaner born in a waggon during the Great Trek from the Cape of Good Hope to the interior. My mother was of Scottish descent but was born in South Africa. My grandfather fought in the Zulu war of 1879 and I had members of my family on both sides during the Anglo-Boer War of 1898 - 1902. In the 1914-1918 War some of my family were killed fighting against the Germans in Flanders and France. In the 1939-1945 War uncles and cousins were killed in the western desert and in Europe fighting against Naziism. I too went to that war at the age of 17 and served with South African forces attached to the American Fifth Army in Italy. I returned from the war to a South Africa that was in the throes of a bad industrial depression, and I did many things to earn a living, including working in the gold mines in Johannesburg. The experience of working 6,000 feet below the surface of the earth with black tribesmen from all over central and southern Africa left a lasting impression upon me: I found out that in moments of danger and crisis the colour of a man's skin was unimportant.

In 1952 I joined the Natal Parks, Game and Fish Preservation Board, the organisation responsible for game and nature reserves, coastal fisheries, and wild birds and animals on private lands. Its function is similar to the United States Fish and Game Commission.

My duties took me all over the Province of Natal, which included Zululand. I served in very nearly all the game reserves and gained an intimate knowledge of the problems of wildlife conservation. I was in charge of the original white rhino capture team that captured and translocated the white rhinoceros from Umfolozi Game Reserve to other parts of southern Africa and to open-park zoos in the United States and Europe.

After reading literature on the American wilderness areas, a colleague of mine, Jim Feely, passed it on to me and we were able to persuade the Natal Parks Board to set aside a wilderness area in Umfolozi Game Reserve in Lake St. Lucia, another state park. Umfolozi Game Reserve is divided into two areas. One is where people in motorcars drive around and can stay in rest camps of thatched cottages; the other section is the wilderness area, which has to be traversed either on foot or on horseback. Over 20,000 people a year visit the game reserve and only about 500 of them go out into the wilderness area. The difference between travelling in a vehicle and going on foot is dramatic. On foot one is vulnerable to the weather and the animals. The motorcar acts as a barrier.

In 1957 I conceived the idea of the Wilderness Leadership School, because I was concerned that the government was not educating people – particularly the black, Asian and coloured people – about the importance of wild lands, soil conservation and the value of game and nature reserves to the nation. It was my brother Gary Player, the international golfer, who made it possible for the idea to get off the ground when he donated his golf winnings from a local tournament. In 1963 a Trust was formed and the Wilderness Leadership School became a legal entity. It was staffed largely by former members of the Natal Parks Board — Hugh Dent, John Tinley, Barry Clements and Jim Feely — men who had worked in the game reserves and who knew the country intimately. In 1974 I resigned from the Natal Parks Board after 22 years' service to devote myself full time to the Wilderness Leadership School.

The concept of wilderness is understood by a large section of the population of the United States and Canada because by and large everyone speaks the same language, English. There is also a long-established tradition of wilderness education and political lobbying by such organisations as the Sierra Club and the Wilderness Society. This tradition resulted in the Wilderness Bill of 1964, which set aside vast wilderness areas in the United States.

South Africa is very different. To begin with, many languages are spoken: Zulu, Sotho, Tswana, Venda, Bapedi, Swazi, Shangaan, English and Afrikaans. Each group has its own concept of wilderness, and the only thing that is common is the instinctive understanding. The black people of South Africa were originally wilderness people; they were part of the wild landscapes and had a deep affinity with the wild animals, the birds and particularly the plants. Many of them were recipients of the knowledge of the first people of southern Africa, the Bushmen, who left us the most beautiful rock paintings in the world. The interaction between the black Iron Age people and the nomadic Bushmen was profound, each giving valuable information to the other.

By the 1890s the whole of South Africa was under white rule, half of it under the Afrikaans-speaking republics of the Orange Free State and the Transvaal and the other half under the English-speaking colonies of Natal and the Cape of Good Hope. In their conquering of South Africa, both the English and the Afrikaner came into contact with the wilderness people, including the Bushmen. In their long trek into the interior of southern Africa with their covered waggons, the Afrikaner trekkers, as they were known, were daily exposed to the wilderness of staggeringly beautiful landscapes, huge rivers, apparently limitless herds of game, and isolation under the stars. The only literature they carried was "Die Boek" – the Bible. That experience of those early Afrikaner trekkers is still very much alive in the psyche of the Afrikaner but has only recently begun to be expressed. There is only a tiny remnant of wild country left; South Africa has become a highly industrialized country.

The English-speaking people have a highly conscious appreciation and understanding of wilderness for two reasons. Many of them are of Celtic extraction and the Celts were a wilderness people. The wilds of Wales and the glens and mountains of Scotland required a special breed of men who could survive the hostile environment. The ancient Celts used to make pilgrimages to the nemetons, the groves of oak trees. They were there to experience the soul mood. This experience is part of the tradition of the English-speaking people. The second reason is that the English-speaking people have a longer history of industrialisation, and this has made them understand the need for areas where mankind can walk, canoe or ride a horse away from the sights and sounds of the modern world.

Between 1899 and 1902 the English fought the Afrikaners for the control of South Africa. Although the English won the war, the Afrikaners never gave up the fight and by 1948 they had won political control of South Africa. But the white people are in the minority, and slowly but surely the black people of South Africa are expanding their political influence and control.

It is against this background that the reader must read the statements of these young people expressed in this book. They come from all races, creeds and colours, mostly from South Africa, although many have come from other countries as well. Their time in the wilderness seldom exceeds five days, of which at least two are required to orient themselves, since 98 percent of these young people come from urban industrialised areas. Most are between the ages of 13 and 18, although people of all ages are welcome to join the trail.

Field officers who lead them into the wilderness give an historical sketch and endeavour to tell the participants where we have all come from in southern Africa and how important our fine wild areas are to the future of the country and to the world.

The classrooms of the school are the game reserves of Umfolozi and Lake St. Lucia in Zululand, the Drakensberg Mountains under the control of the Forestry Department, and a large, 25,000-acre private game ranch called Kampiana in the Eastern Transvaal which borders the enormous Kruger National Park, 6,000 square miles and as big as the State of Israel. The Pilanesberg National Park, under the control of the independent government of Bophutatswana, is another of the classrooms used by the Wilderness Leadership School.

Expeditions – I call them "trails" – consist of no more than six participants and the field officer, and they depart from Durban, which is the biggest seaport on the east coast of Africa, or from Johannesburg, the most industrialised city on the African continent. The format in either case is the same.

For example, the experience of a trail to the Umfolozi Game Reserve might unfold like this. By Volkswagen microbus, the most common form of transport, the journey from Durban to the game reserves takes about three and a half hours on paved, macadamised roads. Once leaving the environs of the city of Durban, most of the journey is through sugarcane-growing country, then through big plantations of eucalypt and pine, exotics planted for their use in the paper mills or as pit props in the mining industry. The cane fields and the exotic plantations carry almost no wildlife, except in the few acres of indigenous bush left by some sensitive owners. Many towns are passed en route to Umfolozi Game Reserve, and a stop is usually made at Mtubatuba (He-who-is-pummelled-out), the small town nearest the reserve, to buy provisions.

The Wilderness Leadership School maintains rough camps in the bush with the permission of the Natal Parks Board, the controlling authority of the game reserve. The camp consists of two tents in case it rains, sleeping bags, cooking and eating utensils, groundsheets and thin foam mattresses. There are no chairs. Camps are placed near the Black Umfolozi River and they are used as a base to walk from each day. Some trails are purely backpacking, where everything is carried and no use is made of base camps.

Trailists are given an historical introduction to Umfolozi Game Reserve by the field officer. They are told about the animals there, such as the white rhino, and that it was due to the white rhino that Umfolozi Game Reserve was proclaimed by the Governor of Natal in 1897. The animal was thought to be extinct until a group of men hunting down at the junction of the White and the Black Umfolozi Rivers shot what they thought were black rhino, but found to their astonishment that they were the white species.

The game reserve is completely fenced with cable to keep the rhino in, and with barbed wire and chicken netting to contain the lion and the leopard and the different species of antelope such as impala, nyala, kudu, waterbuck and grey duiker. Elephant have recently been reintroduced; they were in the area originally but were shot out in the early 1900s.

The trailists are aware that they are in a completely different world the moment they drive through the gates of the game reserve. The monotony of the cane fields and straight rows of pine and eucalypt trees, and the roar of traffic, the stench from paper mills and factories, is replaced by wild acacia trees, zebra and wildebeest grazing on open grasslands, and vultures or eagles flying in the sky. The sense of anticipation amongst the group becomes perceptible. To all of them this is a strange world and there are few who are not afraid in some way or another. It matters not from which background they come, racially or culturally; they all have at some time heard stories of lions killing people, as happened most recently when two game guards in the reserve rode into some rhino. The horses panicked, bolted into a pride of lions and threw the riders, who were killed and

eaten by the lions. Stories of snakes, the deadly black
mamba, the puff adder or the mfezi (spitting snake) are common to all people in South Africa, most of the stories growing
in the telling. Now suddenly the trailists find themselves in
the country where the stories originated, and a silence
descends upon the group. The sight of a white or a black
rhino on the side of the road elicits gasps at its size and at
the conscious realisation that they will soon be walking
amongst these animals and camping out in the night.

The trailists are also told about the interdependence
between the wild animals and the people who once lived
here — the early and late Stone Age man, the Bushmen who
once hunted and lived in these valleys, the great Zulu emper-
or Tshaka, who forged the clans, living in scattered groups
all over the country, into the great embryonic Zulu nation.
The hills and streams bear Zulu names with important meaning. Mhluzi ("soup") Stream was named from the battles
that had taken place, when the blood and gore in the water
looked like soup. The hill named Mpila means "health." It
was a place the people retreated to when malaria and tsetse
fly infestations were at their worst. Ntaba-amanina, another hill (Hill-of-our-mothers), derived its name from the
battles that took place amongst the men on the plains down
below, while the women sat with the beer on the hill above.

The trailists are briefed to walk in single file, not to
talk while walking, and what to do when the trail party is
confronted by a lion or a rhino. The difference in the tempera-

ment of the black and the white rhino is explained, the black rhino being aggressive and the white rhino placid. Trailists are warned about crocodiles in the river, and to drink only water that has been boiled. The toilet in the bush is the earth, and every hole must be dug to the depth of a spade blade.

One of the most important duties as well as pleasures is the keeping of the night watch, and usually between an hour and an hour and a half per night is spent by each individual. It is necessary to do because rhino or lion could easily walk into the camp, as there are no fences or stockades. The person on watch has the lives of all his or her companions in his care.

I have lain in my sleeping bag on the edge of the fire and watched a young person staring into the fire or glancing fearfully into the darkness beyond the flames. The roaring of a pride of lions, the rasping cough from a passing leopard, and the trumpeting of elephant or snorting of a rhino causes great consternation, but gradually the watcher settles down, realizing there is not at that moment any danger. By the second or third night the person on watch could be sitting deep in thought, all but oblivious of animals walking past or owls hooting from a tree overhead. They are caught up in the atmosphere of ancient Africa that the early explorers experienced and that the prophets went out into the desert to seek. One can almost see the inspiration pouring in, and many of them sit and write, trying to record their thoughts, emotions, observations and fears. Sunrise and sunset have come to mean something in their lives, and the now established routine of bathing in a safe pool in the river in starlight is something to be looked forward to, instead of feared. When they walk out of the wilderness area and trek back to the microbus they are very different people. The most common expression is, "This experience changed my life."

Besides giving adults and young people from all walks of life an experience in wild country, so that they will become the vanguard of the "ecological conscience" that Aldo Leopold spoke and wrote about, The Wilderness Leadership School has other objectives. It aims to develop in the individual a better understanding of himself and of his fellow men, as well as the importance of conservation for mankind's survival. These three relationships of Man to God, Man to Man and Man to Earth are represented by the three points of the umSinsi or *Erythrina* leaf, the symbol of the Wilderness Leadership School. It was chosen 25 years ago by Magqubu Ntombela, my friend and mentor, as he explained to me, "It is the tree of the settlements of people as well as the wilderness." In summer, the leaves are green. In winter, there are blood red flowers. It symbolises the growth that man must undergo in order to become whole.

I can remember taking the first trail way back in 1958 and thinking to myself how foolish I was to believe for one moment that we would be able to raise the consciousness and bring about an understanding of the value of our natural resources, yet at the same time I knew that my own attitudes had changed most dramatically through working in wild areas. Since then, some 8,000 people have been out on trail with the Wilderness Leadership School. There are very few of those 8,000 who were not profoundly affected by the experience. At the same time as they were being influenced by the wilderness, personal attitudes were changing; the trails have become a meeting place of minds, where the different race groups in South Africa can see each other not as black or white or coloured or Asian, but as people. Accompanying all this is the realisation that what they have undergone is a religious experience, although not everyone would be prepared to openly acknowledge it.

The wilderness of Africa was the home of original man. Could this be why a 17-year-old boy from Manhattan said, after only three days in the wilderness area of Umfolozi Game Reserve, "I feel at home here and I don't really know why." His comment was proof to me that there beats within the heart of all mankind the awareness that our world is in serious ecological trouble. The Zen Buddhists put it best by saying: "What we need in the world today is to hear within us the sounds of the earth crying." The wilderness experience helps us to articulate "the sounds of the earth crying."

The threats to game reserves, national parks, nature reserves and wilderness areas in South Africa hardly differ from those in any other developed country: overpopulation, increasing industrialisation, soil erosion, greed, ignorance and insufficient finance for conservation work. The biggest difference between South Africa and other developed countries is the complexity of our problems, which are compounded by the different race groups. I believe that those who go on the wilderness trails are not only the ecological vanguard of South Africa but also the vanguard for a different constitution, one that will be unique in the world. It will be a long time in coming but the yeast is stirring. I hear murmurings of it on every trail I take out, and I see glimpses of it in the reports that come in from young people, as you will read in this book.

What of the trail to the future? Wilderness is one of the most precious resources on our planet. Only a few countries give it legal protection. It is the task of everyone who knows the power of wilderness to fight for its retention and to persuade all governments of its importance to humanity.

During one of our wilderness trails, while camped on the banks of the Black Umfolozi River, we came up with the idea of a world wilderness congress to increase understanding of the wilderness and its vitalness to us as humans and part of this earth. We have now had three World Wilderness Congresses — one in Johannesburg in 1977, one in Australia in

1980, the third in Scotland in 1983 — and a fourth is planned for America in September 1987 in Denver, Colorado. The World Wilderness Congresses in their own way have become trails into the wilderness of the mind based upon the profound experience of scientists, politicians, artists, writers and poets. Those people attending know that the congresses are evidence of the quickening pulse of our concern for the world in which we live. They know too that it is not only the scientific factual warnings of unparalleled disasters facing us that will save our species. It requires the ancient knowledge of tribal people, the emotion of art, poetry and literature, religion and the practical guidance of those who have been through the fire of politics. The environment needs a holistic approach in the widest sense of the word.

The principal strength of wilderness is that it is impartial to short-term benefit, or to imbalanced or egocentric thinking. The wisdom in wilderness is long-term and evolutionary. Therefore, increasingly in the minds of people, especially those who are concerned with a balanced future for themselves and their children, wilderness has become a symbol of environmental quality. Many challenges stand between ourselves and the true understanding of what it means to live in harmony with our environment. Perhaps the greatest of these challenges is to overcome the persistent sense of ineffectiveness and the visions of doom in the human psyche. Here we need to urge the psychologists to look deeper into the human mind and to find answers to the paradox of people as willful and destructive beings and people as loving and concerned beings. The reconciliation of these opposites is our most urgent quest. Carl Gustav Jung knew and understood this, and continually voiced it. It is my personal conviction that wilderness in all its definitions is a key to resolving this paradox. Above all, we must never overlook the spiritual impact of wilderness.

I have spent many lonely nights and anxious days worrying about the future of the Wilderness Leadership School. To keep it going has been the greatest struggle of my life, surpassing by far many other battles in the cause of wildlife conservation.

I owe much to the small band of field officers who continued to take out trails long after they were burnt out with the exhaustion of repetitive questions and the psychological and physical stress of being responsible for human lives in sometimes dangerous situations. The Wilderness Leadership School has also been served by a most dedicated group of women clerical staff who worked long and arduous hours in poor conditions and with small pay, ensuring that the paperwork and other administrative matters were efficiently dealt with. Without my wife Ann and her quiet encouragement as well as her participation in administration and as hostess, the Wilderness Leadership School could never have survived. Men throughout history have tended to take their wives for granted, always forgetting that in the darkest hours, it is always the wife who is ready to give support, without questions and without expecting anything in return. To have achieved what the Wilderness Leadership School has achieved, I have had to spend many weeks away from home, in the bush on trails, or in the cities making presentation after presentation to leaders in commerce and industry, asking for funds to keep this small organisation alive. My family life suffered enormously and would have been destroyed were it not for the tenacity, courage and love of my wife, who kept the home alive.

I also owe an unrepayable debt of thanks to my friend, companion and mentor Magqubu Ntombela, who at the age of 86 is still going out on trail with me. His deep and intuitive knowledge of the bush is an inspiration to everyone who comes in contact with him. From the first time I met him when I was a young game ranger in Umfolozi game reserve, he has shown me by example what it is to be a man of compassion and understanding for all people, irrespective of their race or colour or creed. Magqubu Ntombela has always epitomized the nobleness and bravery of the Zulu people. When the Wilderness Leadership School was going through many of its crises, the lack of money or the understanding of its purpose, Magqubu was there to encourage me with the words that we were doing the work of "inkulunkulu," the Great God of all humanity.

I remember once sweating on a hot day in a deep valley in the Umfolozi game reserve and wondering out loud about the wisdom of leading trails at my age and with my creaking bones. Magqubu smiled and said: "Yes, it is true that once we were important men in the service of the government and could have ordered people not only to carry our packs but us too if we chose to. But now we are teachers and there is nothing more important in our lives than to pass on the knowledge that we have gained in the bush. From here new people will emerge in the world, from here there will be new beginnings."

The old man was right and his sagacity and understanding helped me to carry on, and out of the crucible of the Wilderness Leadership School trails have come four World Wilderness Congresses and the formation of the American-based International Wilderness Leadership Foundation, which has encouraged and assisted many young people from the United States and elsewhere to participate on Wilderness Leadership School trails in southern Africa.

Today, after nearly 29 years of struggle, the Wilderness Leadership School is in a sound financial position and has programmes that are attracting racially mixed groups from commerce and industry in South Africa. It is now appreciated that in the bush of southern Africa, on a trail, people can get to understand each other more quickly than in any other environment, and that following the trail there is a permanent bonding. Evidence of this can be seen from the emotions of the young people expressing themselves in this book. They came to understand that conservation was far more than the protection of animals, birds and plants. They have realized that the survival of humanity is now at stake.

The trail to the future lies in the hands of all of us who have experienced wilderness. As I grow older I have come to realize that all I can do is write and talk about wilderness at every opportunity, and take people into it as often as is possible. No matter where one may be, there is always at least one person who is prepared to listen. I believe the expressions from the young people in this book are proof that the wilderness is a moveable feast that we can use to nourish the minds and spirits of human beings everywhere.

God bless Africa
Guard her children
Guide her rulers
And give her peace.

Ian Player
Phuzamoya
1987

Go where no other man is,
Go into the wilderness where
    once you dwelled.
Pay your respects to that which has remained
    — has had no choice but to remain.
Let what surrounds you become a part of you.
Feel the earth beneath
Smell the air around
Hear the vibrancy of survival.
Open your every sense
Become a part of nature
Not an onlooker, nor an uninterested bystander.
And nature will become a part of you,
A part that can never be removed.
Go where no other man is.
Go into the wilderness and
You will never again be the same.
    Cindy Bradburn

I   Me

When we first set off into the bush, I had a "sick feeling" in the pit of my stomach — it was either fear of never having been in a game reserve, or it was the joy of my first trail in the bush. The only times I had ever seen wild animals were either in a cage at the zoo, or through the windows of a car. To be side by side with them in their territory was a completely new experience, an experience which I can never forget.

Brendan Dalzell

Something I discovered was that I must have time to search myself — sitting alone in such a wonderful place, with noises coming from the different animals from all directions, I discovered myself — there was nothing I could do to take my attention away from it — no scapegoat — I had to search myself. I realised then that man has a unique relationship with God, others and himself. These truths are inescapable.

Lesiba Kekana

I felt clumsy and a foreigner in the new environment, but that was the beauty of the whole trail, being away from the rush, the noise and tons of people, just with the sounds of nature and your own thoughts.

Vicky Arnold

It was indeed an education to see how nature has the ability to heal its wounds. While on trail in the Umfolozi we came across an area which had been overgrazed. Thorny, low bushes had invaded the area, thus preventing the influx of the animals responsible for the overgrazing and allowing the grass to revive. I also notice that many of man's most human characteristics are also found in the animal world. I learnt about land ownership — how birds stake out territory with song and mammals by demarcating with a characteristic smell, the rhino's dung heap method being particularly fascinating. I gazed in awe at the perfect orderliness with which a troop of baboons made its way along a ledge. These observations and others made me realize that we are all more closely akin than we think.

During those momentous days I learnt to observe far more closely. The scene was no longer merely one of bush, some trees and a river. A tree ceased merely to be something that provides shade in a city park. I learnt to analyse my surroundings, to notice the transition from one type of habitat to another and to think about the corresponding change in wildlife. In open country I soon anticipated the sight of a herd of zebra or a white rhino. In thickly vegetated areas a bushbuck was expected while a wary eye was kept open for black rhino. Trees I now view with an eye to characteristic features such as peculiar bark or leaves or wood with special qualities. I learnt to identify trees by way of small marks made by animals. In a nutshell I came to know nature on a far more intimate level.

John Counihan

It may seem stupid, but I removed my watch. By doing this I lost all track of time and if it were not for our clothing, I would have felt as if I had landed from another planet. To me there is nothing more beautiful than to relax and listen to the sounds of the wild. You feel as if you are the only living human being and nothing in the world matters. You sort out a lot of things that could possibly be troubling you, and by doing this find an inner peace that I don't think one could do in a city environment.

David Freed

Although I was afraid of being in the wilderness for a week, I must say that I really enjoyed being amongst other people from different nations, towns and colleges. The most exciting part was that I was with Whites. Something I never thought would happen to me.
Millie Belot

I was expecting to spend five days simply viewing animals in the bush. I think I was simply preparing for a new type of holiday experience that I could tell my friends about, where I didn't have to give much or expect any mental stimulation, purely a visual experience. But lucky for me it didn't take long for me to realise that there was something far more important being offered to me, things to discover and learn, not only about ecology, anthropology or astrology, but about life, my future and most of all about myself.
Ann Wilson

It took time to shed my dusty, gritty resistance but as the river flows and never hesitates, so too I lost my city lights and my city crust. I can absorb the sounds, the tremors, the colours and the earth. Life is incredible out here — beautiful. How can anyone want anything else? One couldn't wish for more than the severity or the simplicity of life at its zenith, its peak, its essence. Life in its full ecstasy of offering, providing and receiving. A cycle.

In all this, I just can't see a place for "me." In fact, why should there be? I may know more, but out here they understand more, feel more and perceive more. They exist to the full. I never want to leave here. Here, where there is meaning in simply existing, being and most of all, absorbing. Survival is the message. Still, silent. I don't think I'll ever forget that nyala bull at the river, an example to us all. So serene, as he takes sufficient and leaves sufficient. Excess and greed are dirty words. Self-sufficient and sufficiency are the words. I think the epigrammatic summary of the wilderness creed is sufficient survival. Fear is what I feel now and with it comes acute perception and alertness.

Alexandra Lind-Holmes

No computer can rival a leaf's complexity.
Vicky Barham

While walking in single file the silence gives one enough time to find oneself — an experience of a religious nature, a spiritual feeling overcomes one.
Carol Scott

There never seems to be enough time, and weeks go by as if they were days. On the wilderness trail the whole basis of my lifestyle changed and with it time changed shape. Suddenly there was time for everything. I remember thinking with disbelief at how I normally live — how could it be any different? In the same way it is difficult to imagine that the trail only lasted four days as it felt like two weeks. With this sense of time it also meant a certain opening up of myself to the things around me. Suddenly I felt more alive as I became more aware of my surroundings.
Monique Wilson

What I have learned I'm going to practice, like nature conservation. Many people who live in urban areas use water aimlessly, they kill any creature that they feel is not good living or enemy to them. Like a person who comes across a harmless snake, he will kill that innocent snake. They say they love animals, but I am prepared to preach this gospel of nature conservation.

Joseph Mdlova

For me, the whole situation comes down to the beach walk — walking along the miles of sand and ocean, one becomes acutely aware of man's basic needs: food, water, strength and sleep.

At the end of the first day on the beach, I was more exhausted than I have been before — it is at this stage that the ultimate test comes and you realise that, whatever complex thoughts your brain may conjure up, you are essentially all animal, and as such you are bound to the natural world.

Colin Carus

Sitting alone at the river, walking without speaking, and night watch were all opportunities to journey inward — to reaffirm my values, to keep in touch with the essence of my being.

Carolyn Palmer

I will not litter again having compared the contrast of the spotless nature reserve with the filth of the city streets.

Miles Buxton

This trail taught me more about what nature really is, and left me with an impression of the balance of nature that I will not forget. I find myself trying to find this same kind of balance in my life as well. I am extremely thankful for the opportunity that I received, and hope that I gained as much as possible from it. As time passes, I think I will be able to consolidate more of what I learned, and in turn use more of that knowledge.

Matthew Melville

What happens, is what each person experiences seems impossible to describe. All I can say is the atmosphere, beauty and feeling of the bush is extremely powerful and seeped into me until I felt part of, and at one with my environment.

Monique Wilson

As a visitor to the wilderness you are totally unimportant. So much so that you do not have to prove yourself to anyone since you are so patently insignificant.

A. Story

Something happens on a wilderness trail. I go back to try and find what it was. A change occurred that cannot be pinpointed. Inside was a stillness and I suddenly found I was quite content to be me. It was as if I had got rid of a weight of rubbish that I had been carrying around which I had thought very necessary. My batteries were recharged. Occasionally one can see down a corridor of sliding doors, but they rarely all open at the same time so that one can catch a glimpse all the way through.

Monique Wilson

I experience nature in its fullness and beauty, for five days in my life. I was a visitor in the world of the *Albisia virsicolour*, the *Diospyros mespiliformis*, the perl spotted and scops owls, the abundant herds of the wildebeest, impala and the curious giraffe and the intricate web of the spider, to mention but a few of nature's wonders. Treading carefully and observing quietly, as visitors must.

unsigned

Before coming on the wilderness trail I saw myself as something separate from nature. But being in the wilderness and the discussions helped me to see that I am just part of the ecosystem — nothing more. I have no right to regard the earth as "mine" and to use it as I like, wasting its resources, but I have to respect and care for the earth, carrying out the responsibility of stewardship of the earth, that God has given to us all.

Vicky Arnold

By just seeing the wilderness instead of the city for five days I became aware that there was a God. There had to be a God in all the beauty around you. All through the day you saw beautiful sights. As the sun rose every morning until the sun went down — everywhere I looked there was beauty. As I looked at the stars at night, I saw beauty and I knew that there had to be a God to make all that beauty around you.

Pierre Tullis

The walking, keeping still, bird and animal watching, photographing nature, or reaching a point and taking in sounds, scents and movement in the Umfolozi has triggered a matchless self-satisfaction that is beyond words.

Ronald Mark

Returning to the wilderness was an emotional experience — one of renewal and discovery. Renewal in that there is nothing like sitting alone on a river bank at dawn, soaking in with every nerve fibre and the oneness of being part of the world. The awareness found there is incomparably better than all the information acquired in ecology lectures!

Carolyn Palmer

For me it was a real break through, a once in a lifetime experience, just to be away from science, technology, commerce and industry, which promise the magical push-a-button dream world of leisure, luxury and license. Here I could get back to reality, to true life.

Thabang Mamonyane

I began toward the end of the trail to see and notice a lot more plants, trees, smells and noises than I did at the beginning of the trail.

Eric Downey

I think that the emotional depths that I plumbed reached right into my soul, for I found that I began to understand why I was alive, and some of the duties and responsibilities inherent in my existence. From an intellectual point of view, the planes I trod were most exciting and, of more importance, satisfying.

Vicky Barham

Where there's nothing but wilderness around you and only stars or a setting sun giving light, it's very easy to believe in yourself.
Amanda Hedden

There is time to think, to take stock, time to come to terms with yourself, time to wonder at all the bounty of the earth and time to praise God for all his incredible creatures.
Sarah Eidelman

Once I had taken my watch off, life was heaven on earth. I have seldom been so relaxed and at ease with myself and this inner peace made me much more susceptible to everything around me. After a couple of days I was ready to think about myself and my place in my environment.

Bettina Crede

There were times when I thought my heart was thumping in my mouth. This happened in particular when we trailed and stalked a white rhino mother. I have never had such a desperate interest in the proximity and size of thorn trees before!

unsigned

I experienced the same timelessness as I had before — freed from the fetters of routine, time becomes irrelevant, and one's actions are run according to the body's physical and spiritual needs.

Mandy Cadman

Walking through the long grass under the blazing sun with the wag 'n bietjie scratching your body, all the pretence of everyday life begins to fall away. I found that I no longer had to act as someone, I didn't have to prove anything, nor please anyone.

Ann Wilson

The idea of actually practising self-limitation was completely new to me. At home in the city everything is available in any amount at any time. But now, suddenly a simple essential such as clean drinking water — something I have always taken for granted — became a luxury. This simple lesson could be interpreted as a lesson in conservation of our natural resources.

Barry Segal

Vir my persoonlik was die enkele saak wat vir my die meeste beteken het, sekerlik die feit dat my eie bestaan weer in perspektief geplaas is. Die wildernis het maar weer gewys hoe relatief en onbeduidend akademiese en ander waardes, wat vir ons so belangrik is, se waarde regtig is. Vir 'n keer is mens net weer gedwing om te kyk waar jy in die hele skepping inpas – en die plekkie is verbasend klein!

For me personally, the one single thing which held the most meaning for me, was certainly the fact that my own existence was once more placed in perspective. The wilderness simply indicated once again just how relative and insignificant academic and other values which we consider so important really are. For a change one is forced to consider again one's place in the whole creation — and that place is surprisingly small!

Willem Boshoff

The bush lies mute,
— some men think the bush is blind,
Some men think the bush is deaf —
mute to the ear and eye of these
men who hide behind their iron curtain
of progress.

It feels good to say "I know the Olifants
   River," or "I know the Bushveld."
But of course you don't.
What you know better is yourself, and the
   Olifants and Bushveld have helped.
   Jonathan Bailey

It makes me feel like an intruder on a closely guarded secret, yet even still I feel made welcome. My soul is exhilarated and all troubles seem to have no place here. It is here that I feel at peace with myself, nature, other men, and mostly with God.

Heather Rowse

I benefitted enormously (spiritually and physically) from the trail. The hours I spent in solitude made me evaluate my worth as an individual, and, with a breeze lulling and soothing me, I saw the wilderness through new eyes. As if for the first time, I noticed the perfect formation of each blade of grass and each bird feather, smelt the dampness of the river and felt the softness of the sand. I thought about the importance of each single flower and the function of every minute insect. Maybe I too am just a small creature with a function to fulfill and it is my duty to see that it is well done.

Jill Tainton

The trail did a lot for me, personally. I have always loved wildlife but I am afraid that love was tainted by idealism, an idealism totally divorced from reality. Instead of accepting nature I wanted to change it slightly. I now realise that it is that type of idealism which can be exceptionally destructive. Nature is perfect and the whole of the natural cycle is perfect. To interfere would be to totally disrupt the precision and perfection of that cycle. The human being may aid nature but never must he be permitted to interfere.

Monica Ann Erni

Time was meaningless and insignificant while we were on the trail, except when our stomachs rumbled, reminding us that a mealtime was approaching!

Alison Filmer

The wilderness possesses a tranquility that can change a person, as in my case. Round the campfire, in the silence of the wilderness, I have come to peace with myself. Egotism disappeared and I realised that I was not the bigshot I thought I was. It suddenly occurred to me how small I was, things like getting top marks or playing for the school's top rugby team had no meaning in the wild. There we are all equal, but not quite, because we cannot survive like the animals. We have lost the ability to do so.

B. Smuts

There were moments on the trail when I was alone and felt my own insignificance in the vastness of the earth and the universe. These moments were times of spiritual experience, and in many ways I think the trail was a spiritual experience more than a mental one. I am sure that these experiences are the ones that will inspire us the most to conserve the creation that is so intricately beautiful.

Mark Hurworth

What is life — indeed, and for me it is the sigh of a small wind in the reeds, the grunt of a hippo and the soundless rising of the mist off the lake. St. Lucia — this was the place where, twelve years ago, I was first exposed to the wilderness and it was a moving experience to return.

Carolyn Palmer

I experienced something I could never have imagined. A part in me was not only awakened but was fulfilled — in my awakening I seemed to find so much worth living for; the utter beauty of the wilds; the simplicity yet the complexity of nature — and I learnt more about man and his acts in that short time than I had previously learnt — and that gave me an incentive to improve myself as I lived.

Gill Roche

Something in me has changed on this trip. I feel that I will never be the same person again, and thank God for that. I will go out and fight for our wild country, because in destroying the world we inevitably destroy ourselves.

B. Smuts

My whole way of thinking was changed and, for a while, my whole life, but as one adapts to everyday life one forgets one's past experiences, or rather, one puts them at the back of your mind and you carry on your comfortable life. When I look back, it was an experience I will never forget. At the time it was challenging and sometimes frightening. A challenge in everyday life is hard to come by, especially one you can attack with both mind and body.

Leanne Hamilton

I would like to end by saying "The earth plays music for those who want to listen," and I think that I've finally heard it.
Julie Taylor

From the wilderness I learned more valuable zoology and botany than I do in biology lessons, more ethnic understanding than I do from Helen Suzman; more political understanding than I have from any prominent politician; more technological intellect than I have from my science text book, and more strength of character than I have moulded myself.
Peter Wilson

What struck me very forcibly was the entrance into Durban at the conclusion of the course. After the peaceful, clean life we had left, the onslaught of noise, hustle and bustle of city life left my mind numbed. Everything seemed so artificial and dirty. People's expressions appeared stoney, strained and their movements mechanical. Something essentially wrong seemed to dominate.

John Counihan

Most important, the trail placed me in a situation I have never been before. I suddenly found myself in the middle of, and could actually personally experience, what conservationists are fighting for! I was within the wilderness which is rapidly disappearing all over the world. I could see and hear wild animals which before I have only seen in zoos or from the window of a vehicle, never was I part of their environment, always only an observer from a distance.

H. J. Sittig

My mind seemed to open up and absorb the fascination of the wilderness. Not only did the wilderness seep into my once fogged mind but also the way my companions behaved and talked. I was pleased to see that they also reached to the reality of conservation.

M.J. Whitson

I felt I was a part of this wilderness area and that this was where I belonged; being faced with the skyscrapers and the mad rushing of cars and people in Durban became acceptable after a few minutes, but what I did wonder, and will continue to do so, is what percentage of the people living on this planet today know of their position in relation to nature — do they know enough? Perhaps they are aware of it, but are they sufficiently aware to be stimulated into action?

Chris Charter

The most significant part of this experience was the time I had in which to think. Being out in the wilderness, far from home and the distractions of city life, gave me time to think about my life, other peoples' lives and what kind of bearing I was all taking. I was able to put certain aspects of my life into perspective.

Anton Haupt

There were moments when one wished that time would literally stand still, or when the beauty of a scene before you would remain forever or when you couldn't believe your privilege in being able to be enraptured by the reflections in the water and the slowly sinking sun colouring the world around. These impressions and memories are fleeting and unable to be caught on paper or a photograph. How can one retell the excitement of seeing a pied kingfisher diving for food or hovering above the river?

The wilderness far exceeds any human psychologist, as it is in itself, a form of psychiatric treatment. After a while, I found I had made a mental analysis of not only myself, but of the others — by the end of the course I had come to realize some of the many qualities which make up people.

Barry Bloom

In retrospect, I felt that, amongst those things that I have gained personally, the most important fact is derived from the introspection or self-realization induced by this experience. I feel that, amongst other less immediately recognisable benefits, my ability to function as a valuable member of society has been significantly improved.

A.J. Rydon

The most brilliant thing was finding "me" in the open. Just becoming aware of the beauty and tranquility of nature by walking and thinking and mentally questioning gave me fantastic pleasure; and in that, I saw how man, through his negligence and selfishness, has caused a vicious wheel to turn ceaselessly in nature. I saw my purpose as a small being — to have self-confidence, courage and endurance to rectify those wrongs, not only as an individual but as a spokesman to the masses.

Gill Roche

While on trail, I experienced a deep inner peace because it was such a completely different environment, with little links to life as we experience it, and so simple, basic and uncomplicated that our work-weary brain cells were given an even break.

But it would be unfair to ascribe my tranquility solely to the difference in environments; the main reason for it was the complete naturalness of the bush, with everything being so wild and free, virgin and unspoilt.

Robert Wilson

Here in the wilderness your senses really start operating. At first you just see. Then you begin to look . . . You hear . . . then you start to listen. You touch . . . but only later do you begin to feel.

K.J. Thomson

At the same time I experienced a solitude. Although I was hardly ever alone a feeling of solitude seemed to surround me as the bush surrounded us. It was a feeling of timelessness that is the bush and with it a comprehension of eternity. That we are all part of eternity. This knowledge brought about a feeling of peace and understanding not often experienced by myself.

David Fowle

It took the better part of the first two days for me to properly adjust to feeling and sharing with nature enough to realise that this first reaction was totally selfish and inconsiderate towards wilderness lore. For one must enter a state of harmony with nature and learn to give before one can gain any profit.

Neil Fishwick

Silence makes for poetry of the mind, for recharging those worn batteries.
Sarah Eidelman

It was a revelation, creating a storm in my mind. Something was happening and the process was so urgent, so vital that I'd hardly dare acknowledge it, at least not consciously. An awareness was shaking me and it filled my mind; a persistent mist, not missing a single nook or cranny — every brain cell, every sensory centre invaded. I sat still; so still that I ceased to discern where I ended and the sycamore fig tree, in which I sat, began. We had merged into one being. The wind roared about the tree and I, making us sway in unison and I clung to the smooth bark like some grotesque, misplaced leaf. And the leaves chuckled as the wind tickled them.

"How does this tree view its world?" I thought, and in so thinking, I readjusted my sight and saw the world in startling, new dimensions. The sky no longer receded beyond my reach but touched the topmost branches, filling all the spaces between the leaves with exquisite definition — defining the edges, the pointed shapes, the sharp greenness. There was now no concept of distance between objects. Between the tree and I and the next gathering of bushes the empty void called space ceased to exist. The grass swelled and rippled away from the tree's trunk, playfully bowing and curt-seying in the wind; then rushing into a verdant carpet, clustering beneath spiky thorn trees or taking a whole savannah for itself.

Beyond the branches, past the canopy of shade under which I crouched, a yellow-billed kite hung against a backdrop of blue. My vision telescoped and I saw his tail feathers tilting in an air-current, each shift steadying him aloft. His head bent forward. The eyes glinted as he searched out scurrying shapes which would precipitate that swift plunge to the ground.

Dropping my eyes, I lost myself in the contemplation of the thorn bushes and mpafa trees that grouped along a slight rise beyond me. I couldn't see the game but knowing that it was there — hidden, thrilled me to the core. The knowledge that perhaps just out of sight, a herd of nyala would be moving on cloven hooves through the trees, horned-heads bent to tear softly at the grass, ears swivelling, nostrils flared — never forgetting their role of the hunted. That sudden gust of wind, tearing at my hair and shirt, making the branches

thrash low towards the ground — that would cause the nyala to gather, muscles bunched, ready for flight. Then they would relax and sensing the wind's teasing mood, go back to their grazing. The speculation was sweet.

A deep sigh gathered on my lips and I grinned up at my leafy companion. "I could stay here forever," said the sigh. Forever part of this tree, this blown grass, this pulsing landscape — just content to be. Just being — like the kite pinned against the sky. Just being — like the tree around me, spreading cool shadows across the earth. Just being — like the tender grass bursting with sun-soaked richness. Just being — like the nyala living only for the moment; no past, no future to hamper his vision.

Sighing again, I was content. And in this contented state, the Wilderness gathered me to its breast and nourished my soul.

Unsigned

I did a good deal of growing-up in the handful of days that I spent out in the wilderness. Even now I'm not exactly sure how I feel about that. I'm a great believer in youth; not so much as a physical thing but as a state of mind.

All "grown-ups" must keep a precious piece of childhood hidden away within them for any such time as the responsibilities of being an adult become too much or are pushed aside by choice. For a childlike openness and honesty and curiosity are so very vital if one is to desire pleasure from life's simple things, (and nothing is all that simple to a child).

I grew up in the bush, because of all the adult problems I became aware of; problems that I could face from no other view point than from that of an adult. But, I must have protected my piece of childhood as well as I still have the dream of a youth; I can still gather together hopes for a better tomorrow and a perserving spirit with which to see those dreams fulfilled. My wilderness experience has altered those hopes and instilled in me some fear for them, but only enough to keep them in contact with reality; to transform them into goals that are real.

Unsigned

Visit . . . .
A line of eight
snaking its way through veld
scratched and peppered with ticks
stalking and even crawling on hands and knees.

To the startled amazement of a
long-lashed giraffe.
Then the intrusion becomes impolite
a quick turn, a flash of a paintbrush tail
and away she rollicks
too soon, for the camera-clickers to stare,
just over there,
over a thornbush.
        unsigned

II   US

From the moment we arrived here I knew this was something unique. Many things have touched me. I expected to see a lot of servants, but Kenny has taught me something — he's a man and White — but he does everything willingly on his own. As a Black person in South Africa, this is one instance where I think all of us will agree that we all need one another. I've never seen so much togetherness, sharing, youth and unity. We were just one good, happy family.

Tembeka Gamndana

Where we were, there were few times when we were totally cut off from other people, but we still got an idea of how we need to fit in. Things that seem natural to us are not natural in nature. So, we have to adapt ourselves to fit in with the animals. At St. Lucia, when a few of us went to watch game, we realised how clumsy and noisy we were compared to the biggest of animals. We could not just walk along and look at game, but instead, we had to try and be as quiet as them; almost an attempt to be like an animal again. I realised that I have come a long way since my ape-man predecessors, but I have lost that almost perfect physical control that the animals have. It seems that not everything has been improvement.

Matthew Melville

Without trees
where would we go for
replenishing ourselves.
Without wildlife
where would we learn about ourselves.
Without nature
how could we survive.
Without wilderness
where would we be?
    Cindy Bradburn

The wilderness, at times, made me feel
small and insignificant. Everything interacting
with one another, we humans are just on the
side lines! Our clumsy efforts to improve things
only manages to disturb the balance nature has
created within itself.
    Fiona J. Newman

If we respect nature, accept our position within the natural world, and work with it, we can continue building a world that is fit for all of us to live in, animals and man alike. Until we exercise control to ensure this, our hopes will remain unanswered.

Colin Carus

A trail in the wilderness is virtually a good chance to penetrate a group sense in us and to get to know each other in a short time. I was struck by the discovery, due to working and living together, of good qualities emanated by my friends such as spontaneity, generosity and sympathy which we had ignored before. On the occasion of chatting round the camp fire at nights, a flow of affection ran through each one's heart. After this trail it is certain that we will get along better than ever.

Y Tseng

The sandy water in that intense heat was like a milkshake to us. In under one hour we had totally relaxed and adjusted to the new atmosphere. An atmosphere which is quiet, yet full of sounds; slow, yet filled with action and casual, yet full of responsibility.

unsigned

Having to dig for and use their water supply sparingly helps the city folk appreciate the preciousness of water.

Gail Euston-Brown

I shall always treasure the unique atmosphere of seclusion and solitude that prevailed while on trail in Umfolozi. It was a revelation to have the weight of civilisation lifted from my mind and to absorb the tranquility of Nature unscarred. The silence maintained allowed us to wallow in the atmosphere and strain even more fully from human attachments. Initially we felt strange. We regarded the first rhino encountered with a deep suspicion revealing our city-bred attitudes.

However, soon this barrier softened and we found ourselves revelling in the freedom and peace. Small things are burnt indelibly into my memory — the stirring of life I sensed and the myriad sounds of life at twilight; the inexplicable light-heartedness we felt when splashing about in the river at dusk; the comical warthogs with their erect tails when scampering off — the bitter sadness I felt when seeing one of the grotesque creatures floating in the river, a snare firmly encircling its jaws.

Will I ever forget the restless yelps of the hyenas, or the sad, remote scream of the fish eagle, or the brooding beat of the emerald spotted wood dove? I shall always have a soft spot for white rhinos and the intimate way I encountered these huge leftovers from the pre-historic ages. The man-in-the-street's conception of a highly efficient self-propelled batter-ing ram shall never dominate my view of him. To me he means something more human. I shall remember him lumbering off timidly rather than charging. I shall remember his comical rotating ears rather than his famous horns. To me he seemed rather forlorn and friendless, his head often hanging down in a pose of utter woe. Ironically, his real ally proved to be the small oxpecker which presented us with a classic example of symbiosis when it startled a graz-ing white rhino into action with its screeches.

John Counihan

Nature demands several things —— courage, patience, perseverance, strength and love.
Nature has the ability to give Life and the
ability to remove it in Death. In civilisation
these realities are shielded from us — to be
exposed to them is to be re-sensitised.

unsigned

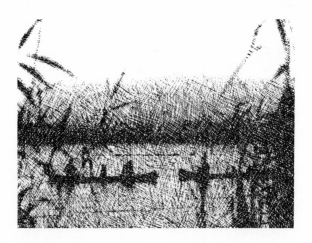

First of all one is brought closer and nearer to reality. The reality that I mean is that of being closer to nature which man cannot do without. Notably nature goes hand in hand with creation which is God's gift to man. One learns to think and have a feeling about God. My thinking revolves on how, what and why is nature as it is. One is made more aware of God's existence and what good he has given to us in the form of every little living animal, insect, plant, etc. Your thinking becomes realistic because of the might of the creator by offering so many diversities in life. Being in the township there is little time to have such a feeling and thinking of reality because there are so many disturbances that put one off the good thinking one has to do.

In the wilderness one also has to learn to be responsible. This was shown by the fact that although we were Black and White, we had no problem in sharing our responsibilities in doing what was necessary. In fact every minute meant that we had to do something for the group and for the benefit of each other. There was no time lost in uncalled for leisure but we could see what had to be done at the right time. For example cooking was done by all of us voluntarily because it was a necessity to eat. Cleaning up dishes and clearing dirt was done by every person who was there and put everything in its right place. This indicated unity, which is strength. It proves that we can live together peacefully with good intentions and responsibilities by each one of us.

    S. G. Mkhonto

Behalwe ons menswees, was die enigste gemeenskaplikheid onder ons God. Almal van ons het God as Vader gehad, en dit was so belangrik. In gesprekke en redenasies, waar ons telkens bewus gemaak is van onderlinge verskille, was dit heerlik om iewers by die begin en grondslag van alles, een en dieselfde verwysingsraamwerk te kon hê.

Except for the fact that we are all humans, the only common denominator amongst us was God. Each one of us knew God as our Father and this was so important. During discussions and debates, where we were often aware of basic differences of opinion, it was wonderful to find that at the bottom of it all there was this same common reference point.

Christo Steyn

What surprised me was that: I did not expect the ladies to be on the guard, individually, while other people slept. But this I regarded as a lesson that we must not take women for granted; much as it was proof, I suppose, that women also have the ability of doing what we think can be done by men only. I, therefore, disagree with these words that say "A woman's place is in the kitchen."

Lento Teboho Josiel

This trail conformed to my dreams. It was gruesome and tiring in that we had to walk long distances in the hot sun. It was nice to know that we, as boys, were able to rough it out in the open wilderness.

Pithabram Naicker

The group found themselves making friends quickly. Social, culture and racial differences were forgotten, and we discovered a harmony unique in South Africa, and which the bush will not point jeering fingers at, as is the case with the world that we had been living in.

This harmony, totally relaxed and natural, showed me that basically people can all relate to each other through nature, no matter what their background.

Robert Butler

How would I have known Andrew Brown had I not been there and felt his personal ideas and openness towards life for us all in South Africa? It may not only end there even outside these wilderness trails if we communicate by means of phoning and cards. Is that not humanity?

S.G. Mkhonto

Mens kan nie in God se tuin speel en onbewus van hom wees nie. Hy het alles met soveel wysheid en liefde, soms met 'n glimlag gemaak. En alles is syne. Ons ook.

Man cannot play in God's garden without being aware of Him. He created everything with wisdom and love, sometimes even with a smile, and everything is His. Including us.

Christo Steyn

Immediately on confronting the wilderness one could but only admire its beauty, but to look deeper into it and understand it, one had to become part of it. I think that this is one of the basic features of trails like these. We as men are only intruders into the wilderness, we are not masters of it. We are intruders into a world totally alien to our own. Instead of the roar of jets we hear the roar of lions, instead of the bark of motorcycles we hear the bark of the baboons.

Peter Hutchinson

Man strives for a more mechanical living all the time without realising the simplicity he can survive in. We slept under the stars around a welcoming fire and bathed in the rivers. Meals which we don't appreciate at home were eagerly awaited. We had the opportunity to reverse the roles of nature where man is the intruder in the world of nature.

Megan Kruskall

For me the wilderness experience has increased that communication. I feel a stronger desire to learn more about myself; more about my friends and the people I live with. Also, and very importantly, I now have an exciting desire to learn about conservation; what is conserving our resources all about? How can you and I do our parts and help others to do theirs? How can we stop ourselves from destroying our wildlife and wasting our wilderness?

Douglas Wilson

Before we can even begin to understand the world we live in, we must understand ourselves, and for this, solitude is essential. For the majority of people, knowing others presents little problem, but few experience the solitude which this trail provides for — this is a totally new experience.

Monica Ann Erni

I didn't come back feeling rejuvenated; I didn't find the answers to all the questions I'm always asking myself; I didn't feel greatly inspired; I didn't find my wilderness experience exactly wonderful; I didn't find my soul; we didn't even see many animals. And yet I didn't leave the wilderness feeling totally unchanged. How could anyone?

Somewhere in my soul something is stirring, the seed has been planted. I am beginning to understand the importance of conservation, beginning to see how far removed we humans have become from the things that really matter, the true things, the stars, plants, animals and the fresh air. So many people have never woken up with the music of birds in their ears instead of the news about hate and destruction; so many have never gone to bed with only the stars above their heads; so many have only seen the grey of the city and never the blue of the sky.

Karen Smalberger

I found the trail had a great effect on the things I thought and did in the civilisation of town. I was never aware of the wonders of nature, ranging from the importance of a tick to the destruction of a rhino. I realised that man is not the "Mecca" of this world, in that we call ticks pests as they make us uncomfortable. We do not think that the tick is a living thing and helps to cull species of animals by spreading diseases.

Myles Buxton

Is modern man not losing sight of his origins. Does he not realise that once he destroys a part of nature he cannot re-synthesize it. Does he not care? Or does he not even think about what he is doing further than if he will profit by it?

M. Goddard

Being in the wilderness was so fantastic,
peaceful and calm. Living with nature with no
barriers between ourselves and our natural surroundings, miles from any trace of human development. Just being with nature and observing
all the forms of life and the land, and studying
all the food chains and seeing how perfectly
the whole system of nature works, was a fascinating experience that I will never forget. I
could have lived in the bush with nature for
months on end.

Roger Rood

The most valuable lesson for me was one in
human relationships — how a group of eight
vastly different individuals with different
backgrounds, ages and ideals could survive six
days at close quarters without one cross word.
Perhaps we were just lucky but perhaps too it
was the peace and beauty of our surroundings.

unsigned

The trail was not merely an exercise in living in harmony with nature, but also with seven other human beings! Life would have been very miserable if we had not all managed to tolerate each other. Although our group was a bit shaky until we felt more at ease with one another, on leaving I felt that I had known the other seven people for all my life. But then, living together and facing the task of survival together, twenty-four hours a day for seven days, one has a great deal of time to become acquainted with one's companions. The friendships I made on this trail will last for a long time, if not forever.

Jeremy Wyeth

That we seemed to becoming daily more empty, lost, soulless was possibly due to the fact that during those six days in the wilderness, life seemed to be so full, so rich, exciting and wholesome.

Sharon Levy

There is far more to the bush than just animals and fresh air. You would have to experience this to know what I mean. My conclusion: "The wilderness is the leveler of mankind, irrespective of creed, class or culture."
Warwick L. Saint

The experience of a wilderness trail only happens once. You may go out on trail again, but the circumstances would have changed and therefore each trail is a unique experience.
J. de la Rey du Toit

Wilderness, it is here I came to know myself, but it was only just the beginning, because I found the more you know your true self, the more you know about those around you.
Janet Shaw

This has proved to me that if people want to live in peace and harmony they must have trust and understanding. There must be cooperation which is the mother of success.

Amor Omnia Vincit
(Let Love Overcome Everything)
Ngoelesh Masitsa

We were seven in number, two whites and five blacks. But the spirit that existed between us made us to forget the difference in the colour of our skins. We lived like brothers even though we never knew each other before.

D. Steyn

Impala Lily

O the blundering hands, the
unpricked conscience —
For, today, I killed a flower.
It grew
under the tangled mass
of browns and greys
of dead undergrowth
on the tidal sands of a timeless river,
this forbidden drop of beauty.
After the first Artist only the copyist.
Nature might have made Sphinxes in her
spare
time.
Or Mona Lisas with her left hand,
Blindfolded.
Instead she gave the grain of sand,
the polished river stone,
the wildflower,
Sunset,
On clouds of pearl and silk and flame,
On a veld of burnished gold.
          Jonathan Bailey

III   DAY

The tangible silence of the wilderness fills one with a sense of peace, serenity and security, even though one is aware of being in a foreign territory. It is broken only by the shouting of a baboon followed by the cry of the young.

Martin Barton

Living amongst a conglomeration of build-
ings which obstruct one's view of the horizon
sky, combined with the fact that I am a lazy
and late riser, nature's heralding of a new
day's beginning and of a busy day's ending is seldom noticed. To actually see and experience a
full day from dawn to dusk and in such close
proximity with nature was in itself a refreshing occurrence. Life suddenly became a precious
event, one which we tend to take for granted
and allow to become dulled by our technological and economic way of living. Time is no
longer urgent and continually consulted, one can
relax and take time to stop and share, filling
one's inner soul with peace.

I couldn't wait for sunrise to begin and to
watch the two dimensional dark shapes take
on form, and become a three dimensional series
of grey shades lit by a pale sky. Suddenly an
artist began to paint all the bushes in a myriad
of colours. The bushes and green trees were
tawny, grey-green and brown with a dusting of
golden sunlight while the birds shouted their
praise for the Lords creation of another new
day.

unsigned

Sitting over my toilet hole I look at my
    surroundings
What diversity –
Look at the majestic trees across the river
The eroded cliffs and soft white sands
Stop and listen to the insects, an orchestra
    playing to nature's own timing
And look at the butterflies spread their
    wings and proudly display their colour
And listen to the birds in search of a
    snack
And look at the flowers — each one so
    different, so fragile, so unique.

Africa, you are beautiful in your diversity
And diverse in your people too —
Men come to marvel at your grandeur,
    others come to rob your rich bosom,
    others to exploit your children
Why is it that men marvel at your rich
diversity of plant and animal life
Yet despite your diverse people who
are part of that web
Is there not beauty in human diversity too?
    Asokaran Rajh

It was very relaxing not to be in a hurry at anytime. The slow and gentle awakening at dawn was a very civilised experience to someone who is used to falling straight out of bed to the loading ramp to send pigs off to market. Dawn is undoubtedly the most beautiful part of the day, and to be able to stop and enjoy it is to be treasured. Somehow the wilderness enhanced simple pleasures, like walking along the sands of the Umfolozi in bare feet, and showering in the peaty water of St. Lucia.

A. Story

I have also experienced something — something that I have never experienced before: that is "silence."

Elizabeth Mabena

Certain incidents are also very clear —
waking up to the sounds of birds. I remember
one in particular, the emerald spotted wood
dove and if I heard it now it would take me
immediately back to the bush. I remember the
shafts of sunlight pouring through the trees,
the fire going and the noise of the rattling ket-
tle meaning it was time for tea and the moment
when night became dawn. My mind is full of
these memories which are almost impossible to
describe and for everyone different.

Monique Wilson

It was here that I first noticed the drastic
change — no cars, no smog, no noise whatsoever
except the occasional call of a bird. At first it
was frightening to think that silence could be
so noticeable, almost loud. It proved how accus-
tomed to the sterile noises of the city I had
become.

Jacque Cohen

The most incredible experience on our trail was blazing a path through the bush and landing on the edge of what must be the most beautiful place on earth. We were standing on the edge of an endless range of white dunes which were visible for as far as we could see, both up and down the beach with clear blue waves breaking about 200 metres from where we stood. There was not a footprint to be seen and the unspoiled beauty of our destination made our long and strenuous walk more than worth while.

Brigitte Owen

One soon changes one's way of thinking in the wilderness. The possibility of a hippo taking a closer look at the camp makes one realise that humans are not infallible and that nature could also do well without us. Unfortunately we cannot do without nature.

Not only do we need the raw materials nature gives us, but also the spiritual recreation we can find in the wilderness.

Bettina Crede

Often I would have liked to have sat down and rested for a while but I knew that we were being led into another paradise or a great little wonder of nature. It was on this trail that I learned that nature could be hard and cruel but also gentle and kind.

Heidi Mutschler

I was wrong to think that wilderness areas are separate enclosures. It was proved to me that man is not the dominant factor in nature; on the contrary, his very survival depends on his recognition that he must adapt himself to his environment and not exploit and change nature to suit his own ends.

Catherine Brutenbosh

Before we went to Timbavati we were blank about what nature is all about, but now we are able even to tell others about the necessity of conserving nature.

Godfrey Ngutyana

I am not a cissy, but I admit that I felt rather apprehensive when I realised we would sleep in the open (with all the creepy-crawlies), wash in the river and be exposed to living cheek by jowl with lions, buffalo, elephants and the like! However, I found that washing in the river is extremely refreshing (it is colder) and it is actually more luxurious than home because the water is constantly renewed and clear and there is no ring round the bath to clean.

Denise Velthuis

Prior to the trip none of us really knew what to expect, but on arriving at Umfolozi I can safely say that we did not anticipate what lay ahead of us. One of the most startling things that immediately came to mind was that what we carried had to last us throughout the week and that our lives were in our own hands. The fact that we were totally alone in a wilderness immediately encouraged self-discipline.

Grant Hubbard

Lake St. Lucia. As long as I live, I will never forget my feelings as we walked through that little forest before arriving at the camp. I have always liked forests, and the forest-plants such as ferns, and the other plants, shrubs and trees which make up that cool atmosphere, but that little forest was breathtakingly beautiful and cool. As I live in a city, I only see orchids in shop windows, but to see them hanging in all their natural beauty was a sight not easily forgotten.
Louise Lagaay

I will never forget the moment we stepped into the wilderness area — the whole world around us was humming with activity; the buzzing presence of invisible insect life heralding the existence of wild animals deeper in the bush. This, coupled with the incomparable bush scenery and the hot African sun, was unique for me. It was a totally new and exciting experience.
Colin Carus

The man who says he isn't afraid of crocodiles is either a liar, or very stupid.
   G. Butler

Something I will never forget is seeing a
tiny tree frog curled under a leaf enjoying a mid-
day nap in the shade. It seemed strange that
such a little creature had found the perfect
place and seemed so peaceful — a way of life
that we spend our lives trying to create.
   C. Smith

So from day to day, we learned that
there is excellence in simplicity; Bruce showed
us exactly what "minimum impact" means.
   I have treasured memories of beauty —
who could forget the incomparable grace of a
flamingo flock walking in slow motion?
   Carolyn Palmer

When I get home, I will have to put two teaspoons of sand into my water and boil it before drinking it!
Peter Wilson

It suddenly strikes you how beautiful the silence is, it suddenly becomes so loud and hammers on your eardrums. The silence is wilderness. You cannot explain it — you suddenly feel lighter — an amazing feeling of being whole again, back to nature. I don't think I have ever felt it before. I suddenly wonder if it is just me or do the others feel this way.
Deidre Marinus

Animals have their own language — their own means of communication. Birds too communicate in their own way. In order to understand them and their language, you have to live amongst them.
Lesiba Kekana

Perhaps the best way to report on this trail would be to roughly outline the contents of one day. Sunrise and the chorus of birds was followed by a warm cup of coffee. We struggled against emerging from our cocoon of warmth into the "fresh" morning air, with its shocking awakening.

Once up and dressed we huddled around a woodfire, dodging the curling, eye-smarting smoke and warming our stiff hands. After a filling and warm breakfast of oatmeal porridge we began our single file hike through the wag'n'bietjie thornbushes and grasses concealing peppersized ticks. Water bottles thumped against our backs and our feet crunched on the dry undergrowth. The day was filled with the grey bulky outline of a rhino or fleeting glimpses of shy buck or curious giraffe who stared at us from behind and above thornbushes and trees. The pathway ahead seemed to be full of spoor foretelling the movements and species of inhabitants who had been in the vicinity.

We studied dung heaps and learnt the habits of wildebeest, impala and the favoured variety of "tree-food." Lunchtime meant a wonderful siesta in the shade of a large tree, overlooking a dry sandy riverbed where we sprawled out in sleep, our hunger appeased. Silence reigned.

unsigned

It is difficult to write down all that I learnt and all that I enjoyed on the trail. But it is easy to write down all that I disliked, as it was only the mosquitoes and perhaps the discomfort of the backpacks as we trailed along with the sun beating down, that I didn't enjoy.

But when we arrived at our first camp at Lake Banghazi all my fears and apprehensions had vanished. It was so beautiful there — we were camping in a clearing in the forest next to the Lake with our own little beach. People would pay millions to enjoy that kind of paradise. But as I sat there I knew that man would ruin it within months with holiday flats and time-sharing hotels, and I realised the importance of conservation and how quickly man is ruining his inheritance.

C. Smith

I doubt if any one will ever equal our record — tipping the canoe, emptying it and paddling next to the others, all in barely the blink of a second. Well, the word "crocodile" probably contributed to this feat. "Hold the canoe, chaps, while I get in." I never before realised that crocodiles have selective feeding habits.

unsigned

After just ten minutes of walking we bumped into a black rhino in thick bush. Until you experience the sight of a black rhino about to charge you, you will never grasp how dangerous these wild animals are. Luckily for us this rhino turned and strolled away (it must have been the sight of my orange hair!).
Stephen Anderson

How shall I ever forget the erect tail of a startled warthog, the rhinoceros timidly lumbering off, the laughing howl of a hyena and those moments of sheer bliss while swimming in the Umfolozi?
Brian Jennings

Then we were "going to collect water." Great excitement! As we approached the beach-like river bed I realised this did not mean scooping water out of the flowing river but something far more interesting. The way the water filtered through the sand to clean itself was incredible and within a relatively short time this filthy pool was providing clear drinking water. Water much tastier than the chemicals which pour out of our taps. And then I was hit by the realisation that there is a shortage of water — and it is not even a drought year!

unsigned

At dawn I sat on a termite hill away from camp. First I was cold sitting in the shade. Then slowly the sun reached me. I stretched out and dozed in a most relaxed way and blissful state. Francolins were rushing around at the base of my termite hill, making quite a noise. This did not disturb me.

Bettina Von Moltke

Although I did not expect Africa to be synonymous with wilderness I did expect to see immense tracts of undeveloped land. In the Bush I felt the respect, not unlike my own, that our guide had for wilderness. But I saw in Africa too, wilderness existed only where man let it exist. Only then did I fully realise the plight that wilderness was in on a global scale — here was one of the last bastions of wilderness with practically no wilderness left. Still so few people realise that when the wilderness has been destroyed in a fit of progress it is irretrievably lost. Wilderness is an integrated system; even a small change in one of its components can alter or end the system.

Richard Maire

On the wilderness beach my first glimpse produced an awed silence — what I saw seemed unbelievable: an exquisite painting to which a fairy had given life. Golden sand-dunes were swept by a sparkling blue sea; the sun's rays encircled the beach, like a mother cradling her child, whilst a frolicking wind raced over the dunes. The beach was deserted — there were no footprints, no people — just us. To me, there could be nothing more beautiful.

Daniella Ollivro

It was with excitement mixed with fear that we observed the puff adder neatly coiled near a rock oblivious of its human visitors invading its territory.

Ronald Mark

As we start looking around I realise that it is interesting to be in such a place, birds were singing in different voices — that makes me happy. I am eager to know or in turn to identify them.

Norman Thabethe

Here the accent was on physical awareness — all the senses come into play — things such as thirst, hunger, fear and survival take us refreshingly back to our beginnings. Physically we were using eyes, ears, smell and touch in a new way.

Sarah Eidelman

Peering timidly at every thicket of bush, creeping around like a cockroach crossing a crowded pavement, dreading every minute that a foot will descend on him . . . that is what I found myself doing in my time of solitude.

Brian Hackland

I turned a corner suddenly and facing me with an expression of utter horror on its face was a warthog. A similar expression must have crossed mine! The warthog wheeled abruptly and shot off into the bush, its tail sticking straight up in the air.

Karen Trollope

Another time a small group of eight rhino treed the entire group. It must have seemed funny to the rhino to see seven people climb this small tree. Masuku didn't climb the tree. He stayed on the ground and spoke to the rhino. He smiled at us and the rhino. I think he told the rhino to get lost in Zulu. He really has a great feeling for the rhino. Close-up without bars between you and beast, the rhino is damn impressive and majestic.

Robert Callahan

Our first experience with the animals occurred only a few minutes after we left the van at our first stop, the Umfolozi game reserve. Our guide spotted two lions only a short distance away. He was the only one to see them, but our excitement was immediate. We hurried to the spot where they had been and we saw evidence of their presence. This baptism into the wilderness really awakened me that I was actually in South Africa, in the bush, and surrounded by wild animals. This new environment was exciting, unique, and somewhat dangerous. I was an outsider in this world of lions, rhinos and Zulu. I was thrilled yet frightened; I was a long way from home!

Richard E. Horne

The main reason which we learnt from the trail was the value of nature to us and how and why we should not abuse it.

A. Jamieson

I always thought that wilderness in South Africa was abundant, but then I did not understand the difference between the general outdoors and wilderness. I am beginning to appreciate why we need wilderness, and why we are responsible for its preservation. I was surprised at how delicately balanced the ecosystem is and the minute detail that has to be accounted for in a conservation programme.

Anton Haupt

We were walking along the bank of the Umfolozi river when we saw a bushbuck go down to the water a little way ahead of us. Immediately we were quiet. Step by step we crept forward. The little buck seemed unperturbed as we moved nearer. It drank, then moved up into the high path just a little way ahead. We stood dead still watching it and it stood peering at us; two parties with such different ways of life, so intrigued by each other. That lovely creature was so surprisingly trusting of man. As it looked at us, it took a step forward and cocked its head as if to study us better. Never before have I experienced such close interaction with a creature of the wild. I will always remember that bushbuck.

Shirley Foyster

The tranquility experienced while walking gave one the opportunity to appreciate the beauty of the surroundings and to realise the need to preserve it. When we came close to animals I was struck with awe and wondered at the total adaptation of these creatures. I became aware of their part in nature and the ecosystem and was struck by man's interference in it.

Grant Hubbard

With a feeling of exhilaration I remember seeing our first game, while on foot — a large herd of impala that immediately scampered away, their tails up revealing white fur, the danger sign. I felt an intruder and wondered what right a simple, insignificant human had to terrify a large group of impala to whom Africa is their rightful inheritance.

Sandra De Villiers

One enters the wilderness with the understanding that one must depend on one's own efforts and skills for survival, and this awareness is conducive to a sharpened sense of responsibility. All too often there are others around us to help us bear the consequences of our actions, but in the wilderness, each man has to learn to account for himself. It is for this reason that a wilderness experience is so valuable for those in positions of leadership, and for those who are destined to be leaders in the future.

Mandy Cadman

It is hard to describe all of the effects the wilderness experience has had on me. I think this type of experience grows on you as time passes on. I remember the thoughts I had as we walked, barefoot, with our packs on our backs, through the Black Umfolozi river. The sun had just set and the moon lit the river banks enough so that we could make out several rhino grazing nearby. Our guide cautioned us to follow him closely, because if we stepped too deep into the river we would be in crocodile territory. The feeling of being a guest of the animals in their home was one that will remain with me throughout my life. I only wish more people could experience this type of feeling.

Douglas Wilson

The course offered me an awareness. A simple example is that before a leaf was just a product of seed, but now to me it symbolises the beauty of creation.

George Pavlich

The experience I had on this trail is both unbelievable and unforgettable. On our arrival at Pilanesberg I had a second thought about being there, but I immediately said to myself, that instead of giving it up I would rather give it a try and that was the beginning of my experience. We were outside civilisation but right in the centre of nature.

Being afraid is something, but being terrified is yet another. We were exposed to an unfamiliar environment and society. To live with wild animals was something that never existed in my mind. But to my surprise, I really managed without being in danger.

It was quiet and peaceful to such an extent that I felt like touching the quietness. I was far from the maddening crowd and far away from the scientific world. When I looked around, I could only see the beautiful mountains, and felt the fresh air that was free from pollution. I listened attentively to the melodious voices of different birds singing a happy song.

I had an opportunity to learn and see why it is important for us human beings to conserve nature. This tour instilled some responsibility and discipline in me. It also implemented some jealousy about the protection and respect for animals.

D. Steyn

The trail gave us all a chance to get away from the hustle and bustle of our modern world — time seemed to stop, as Bruce said: "In the wilderness there are two times: night time and day time, and three minor times: breakfast, lunch and suppertime."

C. Smith

Time was of no essence — morning was signified by the rising sun, noon by the blazing satellite reaching its zenith and evening by the disappearance of the sun and the appearance of the moon and stars.
Daniella Ollivro

In the wilderness time is of no importance. There are no clocks to abide by, only nature's clocks. The time of year, the time of day and weather govern and dictate the pace and order of life in the wilderness.
Dorota Mech

I was not only awakened mentally and physically — it was as though I found a new religion. My spirit soared in its fulfillment and I saw life from a new angle. At the end of the course, I felt as though I was about to burst; yet again I felt like crying in appreciation.
Gill Roche

The tremendous peace and freedom of an experience in the wilderness like this, I found, was a powerful stimulant of thought especially towards the spiritual nature of life.
Andrew Glazurski

The spiritual impact of the wilderness is the spark that is needed to motivate people towards the high ideals of conservation.
Philip Liang

No alarm, no traffic noise, no human noise to waken you in the morning — but the twittering of birds in that enchanting time of the morning when the sun's light drives away the mystery of the night; the shadows creep back under the bushes — time has no meaning and, rather, one must learn to adapt to the rhythm of nature.
Martin Baron

I learnt the pure sounds of silence in Umfolozi and the real joy that can be experienced when one is away from civilization and all its ugly signs.

Brian Hackland

Why did we leave the reserve so soon? I want to go back and learn more concerning nature. God created nature and nature is exquisite unto those who love and care for it.

Norman Thabethe

From late afternoon till well after sunset we had sat in our canoes, drifting with the light wind then paddling. The thoughts that passed through our minds as we watched thousands of flamingos fly by, forming a partial eclipse of the sun, or the snorting of the hippo, were varied. At one time my mind had momentarily passed from this world to the world of nature only to be woken by the "clonk" that our boat made when it hit an "invisible" crocodile! Drifting with the wind enabled us to silently approach a small herd of waterbuck, a truly thrilling experience. Everything that evening seemed magical and "unreal."

Robert Butler

The trail taught us to open up our minds and not to be brainwashed; to look at life from another angle and then to analyse what we see and decide for ourselves what is right.

A. Jamieson

Walking along the Umfolozi river quietly and listening for a noise. Looking around and across the river one could only see the "total environment." Then only did I realise the true sense of these words: "Dam the river and blast the mountain," roared the engineer when told that his highway masterplan could not advance because of natural obstacles. So then it occurred to me that environmental education is the only answer if we are to try and save the last of the environment that is left.

K. Mkhise

Walking through the bush with the wind in your face, the sun on your back and wildlife around you, the most amazing sense of elation overcomes you and you can actually taste the bite of freedom in the air.

Gail Euston-Brown

The wilderness has a way of stripping from your mind all pretentious and false values.

The rhino was interested in only one thing — his survival. To him it was of no interest what my origins were, who I was, what colour my skin was, or whether or not I liked rugby or football.

Colin Carus

It was twilight and the setting sun had coated the water with a shimmering, silver dust. A gentle breeze weaved its way through the trees, rustling through the reeds; a chorus of hippopotamus grunts and gurgles was intermingled with bird calls. Except for nature's music, there was a blessed silence.

Daniella Ollivro

The Bush . . . .

The night
moves through the bush
The bird
calls through the bush
The hyena
laughs through the bush
The man
thinks through the bush
The lion
coughs through the bush

Sound scatters —

Seeps through the bush;
intoxicates the weary mind
weeps through the soul
of days gone by
of days to come.
The soft cocoon
The sharp reality
light softly calls in the east,
And the day bursts through
the bush
always the bush.
God secure me from security,
now and forever.
Amen.
            Jonathan Bailey

IV   NIGHT

At two o'clock in the morning I found that silence is not a time when there are no sounds, but is when sounds blend to form a silhouette of one's thoughts.
Brian Hackland

With the setting of the sun, the cold returned and once more we clustered around a glowing fire that had taken "some feeding" with ant-eaten logs and branches. Supper preparations began in the light of a few dimming torch beams. Potatoes were roasted in the fire's ashes and meat was braised. A shared communal tin of peaches silenced our hunger for the night. A hasty retreat was then made, after fireside jokes and tales had been shared, to the warmth of a sleeping bag. These lay in a row on the ground near the fire and had a clear view of the star-studded sky. There was, however, one unoccupied sleeping bag . . . it's owner sat on a lonely vigil beside the glowing fire embers, listening to the voices of the night. The vigil was taken in turns. Here was a chance to sit still and alone and here was time to recapture the day's excitements. To come to terms with oneself and nature. To think, unhindered by the time or surroundings. A time to listen. A time to realize, too, how man is depleting these opportunities by his exploitation of nature.

unsigned

If the days were beautiful, then the nights were doubly so. The dark velvet skies, high above me littered with thousands and millions of little diamonds. It was then, especially during my nightwatch, that the calm and tranquility really begins to make an impression on you. As you sit, feeling like an island, you can honestly and truly work out your feelings, ideas and thoughts on everything. I think, possibly it is this that really makes you realise that every man, woman and child needs some time in his or her life to be alone and to analyse everything that happens in this world.

Louise Lagaay

Night in the wilderness acquires a character all of its own. It can be as silent as death
itself — an encounter no living being has ever
truly known. A single fire is all that illumi-
nates our campsite. Its snapping flames and
incessant hissing tear open a small clearing in
the oppressive solitude of blackness. Yet the
stillness of our encompassing world cannot be
held away.

All the others have gone to sleep and it is
my turn to take the night watch. Their chorus
of breathing is clearly audible, even above the
crackling sound of the fire. But these noises are
drowned out by one that is indistinct yet much
more powerful, a sound seldom heard by human
ears; it is the sound of silence.

To describe this sound to someone who has
never experienced it, is like trying to describe
colour to a man who cannot see. It is not the
stillness of being alone and afraid, nor is it the
quiet between lovers who have no need for
words. The silence of the wilderness is full of
sounds; a lone hyena's imploring howl, a night

owl's penetrating call or the even, steady rasping of a leopard on the prowl. Yet beneath these sounds, can be heard the silent voice of the person who is really you. A voice that can help you understand exactly who you are and what you might hope to be.

Louise Rich

One of the most exciting experiences during the trail was night watch. It certainly is an eerie feeling and sometimes also frightening, to be all alone listening to the strange noises of the bush, seeing the glowing eyes in the dark when you shine the torch on some buck. Groups of lion were around us every night, from two kilometres up to 400 metres from our camp.

Ingo von Sabler

Tim filled us with confidence for our night watch by telling us of the many instances when lion and other things that bite had come "cruising" through camp causing both guide and others to wish they were far away. Night watch was quite fun except that at first nothing sounds like it should in the bush. Impala sound like wild pigs, elephant like lion and jackal like a nursery full of hungry babies.
Kathy Abbott

The challenging task came at night, when we had to alternate as watchmen to ensure the safety of others in sleep. We had torches only at our disposal and the fire had to be kept burning all night. Nevertheless, my bravado has been remarkably augmented.
Isaac Semiso Tshabalala

The beauty of nature surrounded me on this trip and I was engulfed in it. This was great but there was also a sense of danger. I really felt fear! It was haunting and somewhat frightening. At night I was continuously paranoid about some large animal creeping into camp and taking a bite out of me or my friends. It made me feel small and insignificant. I guess it put me into my place. I realised that there was something greater than myself. Thoughts of God, a supreme being came to mind. The emotional, "mental" effect of this trip is something very personal, somewhat private. I cannot explain all of it now, and I do not know whether I ever will. It was a very meaningful experience.

Richard E. Horne

The night watch was really the most difficult time that I have ever had in my life.
Throughout the day I would ask myself what
would happen during the night; what will I
see during my night watch? How will I react
should anything happen during that time?
Will I be able to decide at the right time to
wake up Bruce for help? I thought that Bruce,
our leader, was going to keep watch the first
night since we were still frightened to be in
that place — I really couldn't believe my ears
when he said each one of us was going to have
a turn to watch! This meant watching and pro-
tecting Bruce himself, the man with the rifle.

The irrevocable time came and I was left
alone, the rest fast asleep, trusting me to watch
over them. I felt the responsibility as a burden
upon my shoulders — the preconceived ideas
that I had about wild animals made matters
worse. Here and there I heard the howling
jackal, the laughing hyena and the roaring
lions. Sometimes, those who were sleeping
were the ones to frighten you by purring. Ultimately, around the fireplace, I said "Lord take
over for I am terrified and weak." In the presence of the Lord, being responsible requires

some measure of confidence and being realistic about your strength and not being intimidated by weakness. The seventy minutes of guarding seemed as long as a day. Fortunately, for the time that I was on guard, nothing did disturb or bother our camp.

Joseph Teu

There was a lighter side, too — the evenings round the camp fire. We enjoyed some magnificent camp fire stories told by our leader who had an unbelievable wealth of experience to draw from. And the evening meals were the best I've yet had. In both cases, of course, the setting contributed to the making of an unforgettable atmosphere. Although light-hearted on the surface, the many chats we had provided some food for thought as well.

Guido Lugtenburg

I experienced close contact to nature at many times. During my night watch when a leopard approached the camp I was completely at the mercy of nature. It was my responsibility if anything happened. It was the last watch and instead of staying for about an hour and a quarter, I stayed awake until dawn. I was so enthralled in nature, the rising sun, the twitter of birds, growing to the gabble of the hornbills and squawks of hadidahs and Egyptian geese. The crickets stopped chirping and the stars and moon faded. Here I could experience nature all around me and I could see the day in the bush coming into routines. So enthralled was I that the fire almost went out!

Ryall Hamlyn

Well the first camp and night in the open with its fearsome noises came and I think no one can say they felt particularly safe. Carol Scott had such a brilliant method of keeping prowling lions off that she kept the whole camp wide awake banging pots and pans together!

Henrietta Van Twisk

The first night was the worst fearful night I ever experienced in my life. I was fearful because of so many sounds made by different animals, e.g. baboons, leopards, bushbuck, etc. We did not trust anyone who was on guard.

G. Nong

The following night the unmistakable roaring of lions could be heard nearby as well as the yapping of hyenas and howling of jackals. The sounds of Africa.

Michael Waltke

Then came my turn to guard. It appeared to me that at that time lions and other wild beasts were now roaring and becoming more vicious than ever. Note well, I was the youngest in the group and it seemed these beasts were aware of that and they wanted to attack. Imagine I was born in Soweto and what I knew about lions is that they destroy and eat any man they come across.

Thabang Mamonyane

The blackness of night possesses a mysterious quality which entices the enquiring mind.
Mandy Cadman

I sat on my little stool by the fire. Listening, ever attentive to catch a noise in the darkness, familiar calls show the ever-presence of unseen animals. I look in the bushes. Was that eyes or the dew? Was that a footstep or the wind? Still I sat as I drank my coffee, passionately yearning for something to appear but convinced of incapability if it should. Thus I spent my short night watches; in excited anticipation and nervous apprehension at the same time.
Simon Dunwe

To sit around a little fire (big ones are not acceptable) on your own in the midst of undisturbed nature is something I've never experienced before. Being the only person awake for miles around, to be totally at peace with nature and to just be with yourself is something that you have to experience to be able to appreciate. Getting to know yourself must be one of the most vital parts of maturing and being totally on your own must be the best way of getting to know oneself.

Debbie Hobson

My first night alone in the African bush was a trip. The sounds of the bush go on 24 hours. At night humans are more sensitive to those sounds. I believe the night sounds were beautiful. The birds were incredible, I never heard such a sound. The bush becomes alive at night. When there were no birds or animal sounds my ear seemed to hurt, even the quiet has a sound I don't hear very often.

Robert Callahan

Before going to sleep you can lie in your sleeping bag and look up at the stars — millions of which you have never seen before because of the pollution of the city. You also see tiny comets and shooting stars which are never noticed at home.

Alison Mason

The feeling of camaraderie which arose from the group as a whole is something all of us will treasure and it is something which made the parting of the ways after the "indaba" that much more poignant. At nightfall especially, we drew closer together for protection and reassurance.

Isobel and Bruce Edwards

What I enjoyed most at night was to lie on my back and gaze up at the stars. Where I live, you cannot see many stars, so it was wonderful to see the whole sky lit up.

Richard Lectezio

Our trail was most enjoyable. We were at one with nature. We bathed in the river and drank from it. For the first time in my life I realised what a lifegiving source water is. I found the night watches very stimulating. It was a good time to think. It was an exhilarating feeling to be the only person awake. I had the responsibility of the lives of my sleeping companions in my hands.

Derek M. Anderson

After serious contemplation and delibera-tion I must confess that Sealy Posturpedic mat-tresses are highly overrated. Heaven is Mother Earth and a hip hole.

Colin Davey

As we sat weary of bone, but energetic of spirit, around the campfire, simple recol-lections of what we'd seen in the hours of that day ballooned into poignant declarations of what we thought about and what we had seen.

Stephanie Parker

In the evening we would listen to the wonderful sounds made by the different birds and animals. We would hear an owl hooting in far distance, simultaneously we would hear a lion roaring, sometimes a hyena answering a jackal in a different direction from that of the jackal. Sometimes we heard baboons making a noise. The last two nights in our camp we were troubled by lions which would come nearer to something like 1 km away from our camp. But because we were night watching they would eventually draw back before sunrise.

Maria Mandlazi

Sleeping under the stars at night, hearing the lions roaring close by and the unearthly giggles of the hyena, the crackle of the campfire, watching glorious sunrises and sunsets . . . When one is so close to nature, one wonders why it is that the general public is so unmindful of the beauties around us and so insensitive to the peace nature can offer, if only we put ourselves out a little.

Denis Changuion

As the others settled into their sleeping bags, I sat and thought by the fire. A bit uneasy, I was always expecting the worst. Was a snort in the night a black rhino charging the fire? Was a rustle in the bush a stalking lion? Would the fire go out? Would the scorpions in the wood crawl up my arms or legs? After worrying about these things for a while, I realised my watch was up. Time to turn it over to my colleague. I made him a cup of tea, shook his shoulder and disappeared into my sleeping bag. Let the animals come now, I thought, I would be fast asleep . . .

Heidi D. Nelson

Sitting in the quiet of the night, listening to the sounds of the bush, watching the flames of the fire leap up, and then die down — what thoughts pass through my mind?

Is it fear? — the fear of the bush, of the sudden, loud rustlings I hear, seemingly right next to our camp.

— the fear of the roar of the lions, that are more than 20 kilometres away, but sound as if they are on the other side of the river, a few metres away.

— the fear of the sudden loud crack of a twig as a buck feeds close by.

Probably! But most of all, it is the fear of the unknown, of the future ahead. The fear of old age, of being dependent on other people. What does the future hold. Will I have a job to do, will I have money to support myself?

I think of our wonderful country we live in, and fear for her. What is South Africa going through. Will the black people rule South Africa — if so will there be a place for us? Not only for the white people, but for our wildlife. There has been enough slaughter of our wild-life, enough destroying of innocent, mostly harmless, animals. But not only are our animals being destroyed. What about our flora? Our lovely indigenous trees that are slowly being driven out by the introduction of exotic plants and crops.

I fear for all of us — blacks and whites, animals, plants — for South Africa the whole.

Is it laughter? — the laughter of the hyenas across the river, which send shivers down my spine?

— the laughter of our group, when one of us leapt up a thorn tree when we walked into a rhino cow and her calf; the laughter when ants crawled inside someone's jeans and had her dancing in the veld. Is it the laughter of our black guide after two warthogs dashed out of their hole and gave us all heart failure?

I laugh out loud, through sheer joy of living, joy at the thought of two more days we still have in the wilderness. Someone stirs in their sleep, disturbed by my laughter.

I realize with a shock that these people are in my care — it is my responsibility to keep them safe. I add another log to the fire, it flares up and I see pictures in the flames — rhino? Or is it lion?

I think of God. Does he really exist? I do believe that in this quiet, peaceful and beautiful wilderness he does live, but how can he live in the mad cities, where no one stops to think, or consider why he is living where everything is rushed, with no time to relax or to even think about God.

Is God Nature? Is he the whole, the everything, or is he "Someone," living in heaven, apart from earth and us earthlings?

Inevitably, I think of me. Where am I going, where have I been? I think of my life, my job, my friends and loved ones. At this moment I love everyone — wishing that they too could enjoy this second, this moment in time where everything seems perfect.

I realise regretfully that my turn of night watch is at an end, it is time for someone else to enjoy the stillness, the quiet and the peace of the night in the wilderness.

Irene Swart

I enjoyed sitting beside the warm fire that first night at the Lake, with the hippos grunting in the Lake nearby — and then, in the morning, awakening to a beautiful day full of newness and joy. My senses seemed to ripen perceptibly in that short period. I was aware of the beauty all around; the sounds of the bush and the smell of nature, the wild flowers and grasses at my feet and the vast sky above, bluer than the sea and at night, as enchanting as a fairyland. I watched as an eagle soared high above, effortlessly, carelessly, with his wings spread and body arched, as he swooped and was carried by the wind until out of my field of vision. I wished too that I could experience the same freedom.

Claire Eathorne

Lying on your sleeping bag at night listening to the lions growling and the hyenas barking, hearing the stillness of the wilds, being able to see every star in the blackness of the sky, and most of all just appreciating being alive and feeling the nearness of our Creator, is to me absolute contentment.

Gail Euston-Brown

I would sit next to the glowing coals expecting a big hand to come down and slap me, saying there, now you are a changed person because of the wilderness, now go out and tell the world.

It doesn't happen that way at all — the wilds carry a very subtle message. A feeling of understanding your place in the world comes over you. I'm not ready to go out and conquer the world's problems, but I do think someday in some small way maybe I can make a difference.

Lori Small

Contrary to the strangeness and isolation I expected to feel, a tiny germ of realisation was already rising through my subconscious. This was telling me it was going to be a comforting and rejuvenating experience. Eventually it confirmed many unspoken feelings I had had for a long time about what was happening to man in the world he was making for himself — but that came later — gradually. I had read some books of Laurens van der Post about the life the Bushmen led in the Kalahari Desert, a life lived in harmony with nature; a collection of the writings of American Indians called, "Touch the Earth," and listened to Bruce Dell, our ranger, telling us how the whole philosophy of conservation is founded on the earth, the very ground beneath our feet. Yet it was not until I lay on the ground that night and the others that were to follow that I began to understand what the wilderness idea was about.

Watching a sky so clear and so crammed with stars and listening to the grunts and snorts of the hippos punctuating the choir of cicadas and frogs; the violence of life around us seemed unremitting. No longer was it "us" (man) in control of "them" (any other living thing); but we were once more on an equal footing. We had no technological advantage, no upper hand. They did not give us superiority just curiosity, wariness and a demand that we respect them.

Nikki Campbell

During the night, the stars twinkling and the moon casting its awesome shadow, I thought about incidents that had occurred during my life, all sixteen years of it, and how they seemed so unimportant but were actually of great significance, affecting the lives of many others close to me. Perhaps I felt that all would resume its natural course, but realised during those thoughtful periods of solitude that unless an effort is made by each individual our contribution to the greater community is worthless.

Francois du Toit

The night watch, where one is awake and alone and must keep the fire burning is an unforgettable experience. The sounds of the wild are exciting and beautiful and one feels a deep inner peace.

Peter Hockey

During night watch, knowing that the protection of the others is on your shoulders, there is time to gather your thoughts about yourself and get to know yourself.

The last watch before dawn has always been the most enjoyable; the coming of dawn is first acknowledged by the emerald spotted wood dove that calls in the early hours of the morning, when the sun breaks the darkness; the enthusiasm of the other birds grows and the sky fills with a light yellow glow.

Douglas MacKenzie

My favourite time in camp was early morning. I lay in my sleeping bag and watched and heard the day awake and the night go to sleep. Certain bird songs suddenly stopped and new bird songs began.

Sam Baird

Night watch was a time of peace and solitude — I was alone, my only companions being the distant moon, the twinkly stars, the animals and the flickering flames of the fire. It was a time of appreciation and expectancy — not fear.

Daniella Ollivro

Giraffe, zebra, wildebeest, warthog and waterbuck all came down from the bush at the same time to drink — not one purposely molested another — each went about his own business, drinking and then moving away again. I thought then that the human race should take a lesson from nature's way and put it into good practice between individuals, races and nations.

D. Steyn

The darkness surrounded me, but slowly a flicker of daylight appeared on the horizon, fanfared by a few birds. Slowly as the darkness faded into a brighter sky, the sounds of the natural creatures quietly died away and the birds replaced them, bursting into full song. The sky now turned from dark purple to mauve, then maroon, red, pink and orange until finally the horizon was bathed in brilliant yellow. Although this had taken less than two hours of my trail, it was in the experiencing the birth of a wonderful new day and a fresh stage of my life that I became more aware of my environment. I shall never forget this!

Elizabeth Thomas

Wild,
Frothing,
Neptune's own stallion rises to the crest,
White water,
His flowing mane tangles with the wind,
A burst of foam,
He dives,
It's gone,
But no, he ascends again to ride and rule the
wave once more,
It's frothing again.

How he jolts and rears up,
To return from whence he came,
To gallop again to rule the waves,
In the powerful, unrestrained exuberance of
total freedom,
In utter denial of chains.

Yet at the beach of the animal,
He dares not show his undaunting self,
his pride,
No white waters, no foam,
For they will ride him,
"Masters of the surf!"
They will tame him, and master
The unmasterable.
        Richard Doyle

V   TOMORROW

For as long as the wilderness is still there, and the opportunity presents itself, man will always be enriched and find deep fulfillment from such an experience.

Panos Lazanar

The story of the Lake is a sad one, which can only be emphasized by a visit to the Lake itself. To be able to paddle around the shores, up freshwater streams of the Eastern Shores and experience the peace and beauty of natural forests, is something I will never forget. The cry of the fish eagle across the stillness of the Lake is awe-inspiring.

The 'feeling' of the Lake seems to enfold you and you begin to realise that this is life and it is beautiful. But against the background of this, I cannot help feeling sad, wondering whether, one day, my children will be able to experience this with me.

Brian Gray

I never want to let slip away from me the wild order, the ever moving stillness, the densely inhabited solitude and the quiet noise that there is to be experienced in what wilderness we have left to us. I want to be always able to look with wonder at a spider's web, with excitement at a baby rhino and in awe of a falling star.

unsigned

Nature has ways of her own to set the world to right; a population which grows too big and takes too much, whilst giving nothing or little in return, will be drastically reduced through disease, starvation, or its own violent struggle for possession of the remaining few resources vital to survival. There is now little time for us to solve our environmental problems before nature does it for us. Although nature's way is merciless and often cruel, it manages to solve the problem. At the present, the choice is still ours — though it may not remain so for long.

Colin Carus

"Civilization" has removed our instincts and abilities to live in harmony with nature. We must relearn those abilities and reevaluate our quality of life. The trail was a gentle reminder of this need and the need to preserve what little we have left.

Graeme Sher

One important thing they taught us — "man to man," "man to God" and "man to soil" — that as a whole teaches how to trust another man, how to trust God and how to keep the soil through conservation.

Godfrey Ngutyana

I never thought that after only five days in the wilderness returning to TV, radio and hot water could be such a sobering experience. But what was planted in those five days won't be easily uprooted and I hope that in the not too distant future I will have the opportunity to return and add to that growth.

Ann Wilson

I really appreciated the quiet, unspoilt wilderness and realised how important such areas are. Not only are they important for the conservation of animals, but also for the conservation of man. We need wilderness areas to escape the rat-race, areas where we can relax and think in peace.

J. van der Westhuizen

Who are we that are so much more important than even the smallest ant! Man needs to
be brought down a few pegs and made to realise
that not only is he shortening his own existence
on earth, but also that of millions of other creatures — and at a much greater rate! Who are
women, that crocodiles should be culled so that
ladies' handbags are of a high quality?
Debbie Hobson

I think that if I had to say what the
greatest thing is that I've gained from my wilderness experience it would be that I'm so glad
that I live in Africa and that no matter where
in the world I go I will always return here to
the stars, the sun and the wilderness.
Karen Smalberger

There is no way I can put into words everything I have seen and learnt, being in the wilderness has been an experience of a lifetime
and one that has definitely changed me.
Vicky Arnold

My trip has made me aware of the many problems that face the wilderness, and how important it is to solve them now so that we don't lose our remaining wildlife and its inhabitants. In the future I hope that I will be able to return to Africa and help stop encroachment of the wilderness.

Frank Lunceford

Every human being ought to have the opportunity to experience the wilderness for we are all part of a common heritage, mankind, animals, plants and minerals. In order to co-operate with our world we must listen and understand it in all humility.

James Mills

The qualified conservationist has already been convinced of the vital importance of preserving the wilderness, he already has the knowledge. It is the average man, the housewife, the school-child, the M.P., the doctor, the teacher — those that are ignorant of the necessity or have lost faith in it. They need the experience, they are the ones who need to be reached, because, in the long run, it will be their attitudes which determine the future of the wilderness.

I am forever perplexed why Man has not recognised the wilderness as an integral part of himself. Maybe it is because deep down inside is the certain knowledge that although the hills are eternal, muscle and bone and sinew are not. He believes that due to his mortality he has risen above the need for Nature — he can now stand alone with Science, creating his own artificial world. What he does not realise though, is that once a wilderness area has been destroyed and a species annihilated, no genius or scientific discovery can replace it!

Jill Tainton

One could reflect on the countryside and what it would look like in, say, a decade. What would I ultimately pass on to my descendants if the present relative indifference toward conservation were to continue?

R. Nuttell

Sometimes lectures seem stuffy, sterile and irrelevant, but the "lessons" of the wilderness are always vibrant and immediate — nature can be a great teacher if one simply takes the time to unwind and absorb her "lessons" which are never sterile.

unsigned

A wilderness trip challenges the soul — not necessarily in a religious sense, but "soul" in the sense of one's set of personal philosophical values, the rules by which one lives.

Karen Trollope

No matter how wise a man may consider himself to be, the wilderness will always have something new to offer him.
unsigned

I think the exposure to the wilderness that you provide can reignite that last desire or rather latent desire for our old natural environment, and spark human creativity to write the poetry or paint the pictures your trail participants are won't to do.

Certainly that's the way I feel. Your trail has led to my being bitten by more than mosquitoes, fleas or ticks; by the wilderness bug also!
Peter Marshall

It occurs to me that the wilderness presents us with a strange paradox. It was from there that man built the world in which he lives today. Now as many (people) as possible must return there to seek the answer to the problems we have created for ourselves.
Colin Carus

To lose touch with nature is to lose touch with the essence of life.
Bruce Broughton

I always ask myself, but can never answer, why can man destroy wilderness with no guilty feelings? What more can man ask for in his life than to be surrounded in a paradise such as Umfolozi? To be at close quarters with animals has always given me a thrill; to be as close to a lion and rhino as fifteen metres, without bars separating us, is an unforgettable experience. But animal spotting is not by far the most important and enjoyable part of the trail. For many years, our parents have paid school fees and university fees so that we can gain knowledge, but the knowledge that is gained on trail is priceless. It is possible to read about the wilderness, but no book can give you the true feelings of love and amazement you feel for the bush when you are in its surroundings. Nobody can explain the feeling that your soul experiences when you confront a lion or rhino at close quarters and without security bars between you and it.

Douglas MacKenzie

I have a vision,
It is Spring —
I see a man walking in the wilderness naked.
He walks with a fell purpose, blending in with
the natural habitat, until he is hardly discer-
nible against the budding background and it
seems as if they are one.

The vision fades.

I have a vision,
It is Summer —
I see a man in a loin cloth hunting in the
wilderness. He is happy and content as a
gourmand as he ingurgitates the fallen doe.
The animals take fright and seek shelter from
the coming storm of extinction. Man hath
broken Nature's social union.

The vision fades.

I have a vision,
It is Autumn —
I see a man in a tweed suit, merely standing
in the wilderness. He stands with his gun at
the ready — waiting — a smug smile drawn

across his pale, ugly face. The trigger is squeezed. His mind delights in the forthcoming food and, in his self-orientation, he does not realise that there will be an end — an end of all his smugness, his mightiness, his self-ishness . . . but at present he is happy.

He looks yet he does not see

He seeks but soon he will not find

He brushes the dying leaves aside, not notic-ing, not seeing, supercilious self obscures . . .

The vision does not fade.

I have a premonition,

It is Winter —

I see a man praying where the wilderness once was. His gas mask impedes his speaking. Desperately he sets his robot to "pray." His robot prays, he waits hopefully, but it is too late, the trees are dead . . .

nature is dead . . .

A tear rolls down his cheek . . . a tear of

hopelessness . . . of desperation.

There is a loud bang.

His body convulses as he writhes in pain

and in agony . . . it heaves once and forever,

grows still.

. . . .

A baboon bark startles me back to reality and for the first time,
I notice the falling leaves and I, too, pray —
Pray that man will realise that he is an animal and as such,
He must abide by the laws of nature in as much as he must not destroy God's creation,
For thereby he will bring about his own extinction.
Amen.
Francis Fincham

I expected to be driven to my physical extent during the day and terrified at night.

My expectations were obviously not fulfilled. Why then was it a week never to be forgotten? It seems ironic but I'm sure my mind was far more active than my body. The animals and simply walking through the wilderness were like trigger actions, setting my mind off: asking myself questions. While walking through the wilderness the question of life and what it is all about kept attacking me like hundreds of ants.

David Trafford

At last I had a chance to think of something new. It gave my mind a spring cleaning and another track to run along. I saw that man was following his own mind and making a mess of nature where he thought he was doing right. If man followed nature's pattern of how she coped with things, surely we would live in a much better world. God made nature, so surely it is right. Man doesn't have to go right back to primitive ways but to apply nature's way to them.

Bernadine Sansom

Apart from the beautiful scenery, game and the marked contrast between city and bush, there is a strong message behind the trips made by the Wilderness Leadership School. The message is the importance of the conservation of the wilderness areas — not only the wilderness areas but conservation of all our natural resources.

Derek M. Anderson

The beauty of the wilderness and the challenges it set forth are memories I'll cherish forever. My ultimate goal in life wasn't determined out there but it did begin to take shape. Wherever my life leads me there is one thing I'll always yearn for. The night we trekked the Black Umfolozi River with a full moon overhead shimmering upon us in a hypnotic and breathtaking silence.

Lori Small

Is man the only mourner of wilderness
because he is the only killer?
Could we create if we could not destroy?
Would we want knowledge without control?
Beauty without rape?
Do I have nothing to blame but the genes in
my own body?
Is pastoral man a half-man and
love a fiction?
Was I just born too late?

Jonathan Bailey

I walked down the street in Johannesburg. I was jostled from the left and bumped from the right. The pavement was packed with people; all rushing, bumping, pushing, muttering. Old ladies, walking slowly, carefully; braving the streets only because they needed to buy more food to feed themselves in their dark flat on the eleventh floor.

Between the pavements, the vehicles roared. Every driver cursing the driver in front for driving too slowly and cursing the driver behind for driving on his tail. Neglected brakes squealed, tires skidded, hooters sounded in unmelodious keys. People on foot darted between the cars, mothers dragged unwilling children across intersections as cars waited, lined up, ready to roar into life as the green signal appeared.

I stood at the intersection, waiting, because the red man was flashing his unspoken, impersonal signal at me. Then as I waited, into that concrete metal, plastic and tar world drifted a pigeon. It hung on the polluted air then flapped its wings to alight on a ledge of a building.

My thoughts went back to the time I saw the fish eagle drifting above the Umfolozi River. Its eyes were sharp, surveying the scene below. On the bank of the river, a group of impala were drinking; ever alert, looking around.

A special type of quiet prevailed. In the distance, the undulating hills were a blue haze. The sky was clear and the day was still. As I sat on the branch of a tree just outside camp, a peace came over me which I have never experienced in the city. All around me were things that man had not yet had the chance to spoil. The trees and bushes were there because of the seeds that Nature had planted.

Shirley Foyster

I know now that without our unique bush-veld I could not survive. I need the silence and feel that this beautiful landscape is vital to our community.

Francois du Toit

I found the trail an experience from which I grew. It is difficult to put down in words exactly what happened, but I feel it has taken me one step further to becoming a whole person. For this alone, I am grateful.

Sandy Lowitt

I wish that I was still there, ticks, discomfort and all. I can only hope that I am learning to be a humble human, respectful of the wilderness.

Kim Woods

How is a child ever going to be able to appreciate the natural world, when from the very moment he can reason, he is taught that all of its inhabitants, from insects to elephants, are his deadly enemies? Do we picture a forest as a dark forbidding place, or as a quiet green sanctuary from civilisation?

This is the accomplishment of the Wilderness Leadership School. It takes people out of perhaps the only environment they have ever known and shows them that the natural world is not only something very beautiful, but something that we are as much a part of as the animals. Enlightened people will be far less apathetic when they hear that an estuary, a sanctuary for thousands of birds, is being drained, or that the elephants of East Africa, and the whales of the world are being killed at an unprecendented rate.

Many people will never visit a wilderness area. However, I feel that it is psychologically imperative for them to know that these wilderness areas, these places of escape, still exist. Perhaps, in summary, it can be said that the Wilderness Leadership School simply makes us slow down for a short time and helps us to appreciate the things that God has made, more than the things that man has made.

James Hallinan

Dis omdat ons in son grootmate uít pas is met die natuur se eenheid, dat ons nou sukkel om byvoorbeeld tussen wit en swart — een spesie — harmonie te behou.

It is because we are, to such an extent, out of step with nature's unity that we find it so difficult to maintain harmony between Black and White — and between species.

Christo Steyn

I wanted to run away from man's world, to hide in this shelter of wilderness that I had so recently been introduced to. For what could I, a grain of sand compared to time, a single droplet in relation to space, what could I possibly contribute to a scheme for a better world? And them I remembered the spark that had been kindled (or rekindled) within myself, the love I had for the wilderness after only catching a glimpse of it. If I could convey even a fraction of the influence my experience had on me to others, I'm sure I could get them just as concerned about our future as I am.

unsigned

What I noticed is that leadership is the ability to make things happen — to act in order to help others work in an environment, within which each individual serving under the leader finds himself encouraged and stimulated to a point where he is helped to realize his fullest potential to contribute meaningfully. It is true that leadership is a quality, provides vision, exercises faith, seeks for effectiveness and provides direction.

Joseph Teu

I learnt to be aware of others on trail — living with the same people in the bush for six days, I realised that some of the world's basic problems would be solved if people were more aware of those around them and of their needs.

John Stathaulis

If our top businessmen and political leaders were required to spend some time in the wilderness and to be exposed to themselves, maybe we would find ourselves destroying less and saving more.

Douglas Wilson

Wilderness is also a great equaliser when it comes to differences between races, ages and even nationalities. On a trail such as this one, we found that when everyone is involved with the welfare and safety of every other member of the group, you become knit into a team, in which every member has a part to play.

M. G. Wise

As the trail ended we all sat quietly. We had all learnt something.

Was it from the observation of animals living harmoniously in nature?

Was it from being exposed to nature's grandeur?

Was it from being disciplined, learning that we weren't master of the wilderness but just intruders?

All these questions remain unanswered, yet we know that we have changed; we have all learnt something from this new and exciting experience.

    unsigned

    To enter a wilderness area which is unspoilt by man makes one feel greatly privileged. This automatically instills a love of nature into every person who comes into contact with it. There is never a feeling of loneliness because one is at peace with the wilderness.

    Peter Hockey

The trail was an opportunity to meet some different people; to discover aspects of the friends I'd known a long time, but never under these circumstances; and to learn new things about the wilderness — and during the time spent walking, the hours of night watch, and a two hour solitary meditation on the last morning — there was time to think about these things and the impact they would make on my usual lifestyle, and myself as a person.

Hazel Tatham

Ek was baie skepties oor die veelrassige aspeck van die onderneming. Nie omdat ek moeilik oor die weg kom met verskillende volksverteenwoordigers nie, maar omdat die noodwendige politiek-gesels en krapperigheid my baie katvoet laat wees het. Om eerlik te wees; as dit nie vir die Timbavati aspek, die geleentheid om in die wildernis te kon wees, sou ek beswaarlik ingewillig het.

Ek was totaal verras (beskaamd, meer). Die mate van maatswees en samehorigheidsgevoel wat hier van die derde dag onderons geheers het, is iets wat ek nooit tussen wit en swart (persoonlik) beleef het nie. Ek kan vir die eerste keer se dat ek swart vriende gemaak het. En dit is nie dat ons mekaar se rue gekrap het nie — as daar gepraat is, is daar kaalkop gesels en is die turks-vye ook nadergesleep.

I was very skeptical concerning the multiracial aspect of the undertaking. Not because I find it difficult to get on with members of other race groups, but because the inevitability of political discussions put me on my guard. To be honest, if it were not for the Timbavati (wilderness) aspect, I would have had difficulty in consenting to participate.

I was totally surprised (ashamed even). The degree of camaraderie which existed amongst us from the third day, is something which I have personally never experienced between Black and White before. For the first time I made Black friends — and this was not because we complimented one another either, for when we talked, it was with all honesty, saying what we really felt.

Christo Steyn

Yet again I realised that life in the wilderness releases inhibitions and creates a person without "hang-ups" and without a facade with which to face the world.

unsigned

From man's present behaviour I conclude that he destroys what is a threat to his total supremacy instead of adapting so that every life can have an equally fair chance of living under this life-giving sun of ours.

To try and discuss all my spiritual gains would be an extremely difficult plight but in conclusion the question I would like to pose is, With nature supplying all our needs is it really necessary to kill just so that supremacy and prestige may be boosted? Surely not and here we have the paradox of the fertility of nature and the futility of war.

George Pavlich

As ecology tries to teach us . . . everything affects everything else and once again Donne comes to mind, "I am involved in all mankind."

Stella Harvey

Now the things I learned about this expedition is that men can stay with animals. That nature can bring different types of people with different backgrounds together and make them think the same way and make them one as if they came as one. I never thought that Afrikaans-speaking people and Black people would ever meet on an occasion like this and come back acknowledging each other as brothers.

Thabang Mamonyane

The highlight of the trail, for me, was the "solo" on the last day. I went onto the far bank of the river with my binoculars and bird book. I found a place to sit and for a while it was as though I was the only person in the world. I saw tons of birds, identifying some. I saw a squirrel and it was so close that I could have touched it. But these were not what made the experience so perfect. I do not think that I could, even if I wanted to, explain it, for it was so personal and unique that to write it would be impossible for me and the true meaning would be lost in a jumble of badly put words. But I will say that I shall never forget it, it will remain in my heart forever. What I learnt perhaps in time I will be able to pass on to others, so that they too may share what the wilderness shared with me.

Tracy Warburton

For more information, write:

> Wilderness Leadership School
> P.O. Box 53058
> Yellowwood Park 4011
> Natal
> South Africa

There are many fine wilderness experience programmes located throughout the world. For more information on these, write:

> The International Wilderness
> Leadership Foundation
> c/o
> Fulcrum, Inc.
> 350 Indiana Street, #510
> Golden, Colorado 80401
> USA